SPIRIT OF THE WESTERN WAY

Wake Up to Your Power —
Heal the Collective Consciousness of the Western Mind

through Tina Louise Spalding

Other Books by
Tina Louise Spalding

Great Minds Speak to You

Making Love to God

Jesus: My Autobiography

Love and a Map to the Unaltered Soul

SPIRIT OF THE WESTERN WAY

Wake Up to Your Power —
Heal the Collective Consciousness of the Western Mind

through Tina Louise Spalding

Copyright © 2016 by Tina Louise Spalding
All Rights Reserved.

No part of this book may be used or reproduced in any manner without prior written permission from the publisher, except in the case of brief quotations embodied in critical reviews and articles.

The scanning, uploading, and distribution of this text via the Internet or any other means without the permission of the publisher is illegal and punishable by law. Please purchase only authorized electronic editions, and do not participate in or encourage piracy of copyrighted materials. Your support of the author's rights is appreciated.

For information about special discounts for bulk purchases, please contact Light Technology Publishing Special Sales at 1-800-450-0985 or publishing@LightTechnology.net.

The information herein is for educational purposes only. The content of this book should not be used to give medical advice or to prescribe any form of treatment for physical, emotional, or medical problems without the advice of a physician. Should you use any recommendations in this book for yourself or others, the channel, compilers, and publisher assume no responsibility for your actions.

The views and opinions expressed herein are those of the author and do not necessarily reflect those of the publisher.

ISBN: 978-1-62233-051-5

PO Box 3540
Flagstaff, AZ 86003
1-800-450-0985
1-928-526-1345
www.LightTechnology.com

This book is dedicated to all those people who have helped me along this most unusual path: Thanks to Alexandria King for her friendship and constant support. Thanks to my sons, Alex and Kieran, for their presence in my life. Thanks to Kenneth Berrentzen and Jenny Andrews for technical and emotional support. Thanks to James Strohl and Laurel Leland for inviting me to go on the road for the first time to test out my channeling wings. Finally, thanks to all the readers of and subscribers to my work. The great feedback and ongoing interest keeps me working toward our collective goal of attaining peace in our minds and on our planet. Thanks to you all!

Contents

Preface xiii

Introduction xv

CHAPTER 1

You Are Not Designed to See the Big Picture 1

   You Are Not a Physical Being...................................... 2

   You Created Your World 4

   Realize the Truth 5

   The Dream 7

   The Warped Feedback System..................................... 8

CHAPTER 2

The Split Mind Cannot See Truth............................ 13

   Western Society Is Founded on Misteachings............ 14

   Higher Mind and Ego Mind 16

CHAPTER 3

Break Free from Your Prison 21
Your Body Doesn't Limit You 25

CHAPTER 4

Understand Your Chakras 27
Monitor Your Energetic Condition 29

CHAPTER 5

Nutrition for the Spiritually Minded 33
Meat and Dairy 33
Practice Patience in Adjusting Your Diet 36
Eat Natural Foods 38
The Nonphysical Realm Can Help 40
Identify Your Fears 41

CHAPTER 6

Recondition Your Mind about Food 45
Pay Attention to Your Feelings 46
Know Making Changes Will Become Easier 48

CHAPTER 7

Release Addictions to Find Freedom 51
Don't Medicate Your Guidance System 52
The Body Adjusts to Your Appetites 53
Addictions Arise to Lead to Awareness 55

CHAPTER 8

Reconsider Your Mind's Nutrition 57

The Past Isn't the Way to a Better Future 58

Embrace Your Special Gifts 60

Educate Yourself about Your Passion 63

CHAPTER 9

Books, Television, and Films
as Nutrition for the Mind 67

Television Feeds the Consumer Mentality 69

Seek Entertainment in Other Places 70

Violent Films Fuel the Ego Mind 71

Romance Movies Reinforce the Myth of Love 73

Choose Entertainment That Supports Growth 74

CHAPTER 10

Change Your World by Changing Your Mind 77

Love the Unlovable Projections of Your Mind 79

Take Back Your Power 80

Separation Is an Illusion 82

CHAPTER 11

The Fallacies of
Western Religious Thought 85

The Evolution of the Christian Church 86

Reject Sacrifice, Martyrdom, and Suffering 89

Explore Your Personal Connection with God 90

Stand Up for Yourselves 91

Align with Love 92

CHAPTER 12

Everything Is Connected 97
Allow the Oneness of Energy 98
Integrate Science and Spirituality............................ 100
Adopt a Holistic Approach to Life 101

CHAPTER 13

Experience True Wealth and Freedom.................... 105
Invest in Your Life...................................... 106
Support Businesses and Organizations
You Believe In...................................... 108
Align with Nature's Generosity............................... 109

CHAPTER 14

Stop Judging the Body 111
Your Body Is a Vehicle 113
Focus on Activities That Bring Happiness............... 115

CHAPTER 15

Transform Your Destiny 117
Make the Effort to Shift........................... 118

CHAPTER 16

Use Technology to Inspire Others 121
Put Your Phone Away................................. 122
Spread Beauty Through Technology 123

CHAPTER 17

Create Space for the Divine 125
Find Activities That Reinforce Change 128

CHAPTER 18

Secrets Do Not Serve You 131
Have Compassion for Others and Yourself 132

CHAPTER 19

You Are Magnificent 137
Your Consciousness Is Reality.................................. 138
Change Your Focus to the Nonphysical 140

CHAPTER 20

The Choice Is Yours 143

About the Author 147

Preface

I began channeling this book about two years ago while I was channeling *Jesus: My Autobiography*. Writing Jesus's autobiography was a very challenging, joyful, and at times intimidating project, so when I could not face the implications and responsibility of working on his life story or just had to take a breather, I would channel and work on the early chapters of *Spirit of the Western Way*.

My growing understanding of Jesus's work and teachings took on a momentum all its own, and this book was channeled and written in the quiet times when I had to process or adjust to my ever-expanding journey with the work. This material became an amazing compilation of information about our society, our minds, and our bodies that became increasingly important to share. I am asked about these subjects all the time as I continue to channel, teach, and work with this material, and I realized that now is the time to get this fifth volume from Ananda into your hands.

We do many things in this society that keep us from Spirit, and we have no clue, most of the time, what those things are because they are normal in our Western world. Everyone, or almost everyone, does them. This book has been a great solace to me over the past two years, providing tremendous help in understanding our world and how to navigate it. I hope you find comfort within its pages just as I have, and I hope it helps you make healthy and healing choices that lead you on your pathway Home to love and peace.

Tina Louise Spalding, 2016

Introduction

We are Ananda, a group consciousness. We are here as beings of light to work with you in raising your frequency from the realms of fear, shame, and guilt that you have been helped into by the hierarchical structures of your society. Your Western civilization has been manipulated for a very, very long time into negative, low-frequency manifestations and structures of control, limitation, fear, and judgment. You must understand the process of creation and your part in this grand play that is expressing itself through the collective consciousness of your planet. We bring you basic teachings about reality: what it is, where you come from, why you are here, what your body is, how you get sick, why you thrive, and more. We address, systematically and in detail, the structures of your society and your mind that work against you.

These are important teachings of things you must know about yourself so that you can put into practice some of the higher teachings that will come through about unconditional love and forgiveness. These higher-frequency shifts and changes are difficult to attain unless you know what has been inflicted on you and what choices you are making and how they affect you.

This book describes the systematic and problematic features of your mindset and the society that your collective consciousness is manufacturing so that you can change them. You cannot change anything until you first see it, accept that it is so, and then, in awareness, shift your consciousness. Until you know what has been done to you, until you know what parts of your society are harmful to you and to your spiritual evolution, you are stuck.

This book is brought to you by many beings of high frequency who love you and your society very much. We have been assigned the spiritual practice to bring these teachings through this being so that we can help point you in the correct direction and you can find your way Home. Home is heaven. Home is love. Home is peace. Home is a world that is a wonderful place to live in. This is not the only reality there is. There are many others, but this is the reality you must deal with for now, and that is what we are here to help you do. We are here to help you understand what is happening and assist you in the reeducation of your mind.

We are Ananda. We are your friends, your teachers, and your fellow travelers on this most magnificent journey into consciousness, and we hope you enjoy this book.

CHAPTER 1

You Are Not Designed
to See the Big Picture

Your body is a manifestation of mind. It is not a thing that creates you; rather, you have created your body. Your body comes from thought, belief, and both truth and untruth. It is the physical manifestation of all that you think you are. This is a large concept for the Western mind to comprehend, for you think that the body is who you are in the sense that it contains you, it creates you, and it houses your brain and all the nerves and synapses that give you your reality. But that is not the case.

Your reality creates the body; your mind creates the body. It is not until you understand this concept that you can really come to terms with your relationship with the body. Your natural home is not on this physical world. It is not in this three-dimensional existence you call your life. Your real home is in the nonphysical. The majority of your self always resides in the nonphysical and only sends small snippets of itself into physical manifestation to collect and retrieve information and to create.

Your real self is nonphysical in nature. It is connected to what you call God, to the source of benevolence that guides all things that you do and do not see. Understand that there are many worlds, dimensions, universes, and realities that you are not in touch with, that you are not even aware of. Your three-dimensional world, and indeed your body, is just a small snippet of reality. You are as a small mouse trying to understand a great city, and it is impossible for you to do. It does not mean that the city

2 * Spirit of the Western Way

does not exist, but the mouse is unable to comprehend anything about it. It does not even see it, for its senses are not designed to see it.

That is the case with you. You are not designed to see all that is going on. You are designed to focus your attention, albeit a small part of who you are, on an experience. That is what the body is used for. It is used to collect and interpret physical information so that you can have a very specific experience. Through the physical experience, you come to understand what and who you are and what you are not. The body is not who you are.

This is the biggest misconception people in the Western world have. You are convinced you are a body. You are convinced that the body makes up who you are. This is not your fault, for it is what you are taught in the scientific method in your scientific and secular world. The separation from spirituality that you have called religion was an important one, for religious dogmas and doctrines were as inaccurate as the scientific dogma.

We are here to teach you a new truth; it is not a dogma. The truth is that you are both a spiritual and a physical being. You are divine consciousness manifested temporarily in a physical body designed only to show you that which is untrue, that which is not who you are. When you come to a true understanding of what you are, you will no longer need to have a physical body in the sense that you experience it now. You will return to the nonphysical and to your true self, which is spiritual and divine in nature and completely aware of its oneness with divine nature and of your oneness with all other things. You will be completely aware of love as your Creator, as your self-expression.

As you look around your world, you see that love is not what is expressed here. You catch glimpses of it occasionally when you hold a baby in your arms or gaze into the eyes of your lover, but it is a very rare and elusive thing in this world. The body plays a part in that.

You Are Not a Physical Being

What is this body you live in? It is a manifestation (albeit a very complicated and well functioning one) of what you are not. You are not a physical being whatsoever, and this is where your difficulty lies in the Western world. You are taught, of all things, that you are a physical being, so you seek physical remedies for sicknesses. You seek physical pleasures for gratification. You seek physical relationships to soothe your separation anxiety and your loneliness. Because you labor under this misperception that you are a physical being, you keep seeking in the physical world that which you feel you need in order to be happy.

This is the first lesson: You are not a physical being. You are housed in a physical body as an example of that which is untrue about you, so when you believe in the body, that it is who you are, you reinforce the untruth, and you suffer. These are the feelings of separation and loneliness many of you have in the Western world. You are spiritual in nature, and it is only in turning inward and seeking spiritual connection with your self, the Divine, and other beings that you will find your source of peace and connect to the never-ending flow of love that is offered to you. Your belief in the body causes you to become confused and misdirects your focus.

Now, the Western mind does not like these concepts, so we ask you to bear with us, for the language we speak to you will feel foreign, as if it goes against everything you have learned, and it might remind you of old religious doctrines that upset you or that you do not believe in or support because the teachings seemed dangerous and narrow. Bear with us a little while, and we will explain further. We will take you deep into a journey through the body and explain to you exactly what is happening and why it is such a difficult subject for you to wrap your minds around, so to speak.

When you were in the divine form that you consider spirit (the form you will return to after your physical incarnation), there was an aspect of you that had an untrue idea. You might consider it the fall from grace that is described in the Bible story of Adam and Eve. It is a metaphor, a mythology, described in that story. There was an aspect of mind that made a mistake and believed it, and because you have a divine creative nature and an incredible creative power — and because you are an aspect of divine mind manifested — you created a world within your mind that supported this belief.

When you came into this world, this is what you created. You became frightened, for you felt a sense of separation for the first time. You felt a sense of fear for the first time, and you knew in your heart that you had done it to yourself. You began to run around in fear, trying to shore up your world so that you could feel safer because you felt as if you had torn yourself asunder from the very source of your being. In some ways, that is exactly what happened, for you believed it to be so. In reality, you never left, but you believed you had, and as you have seen, when humans believe something is true, it is very difficult to convince them otherwise. As you fell deeper and deeper into this belief, running around trying to protect yourself and shoring up your fears, you made a deeper trench into which you fell.

This trench is your incarnational history. It is your life now and all your past lives. These are the ideas manifesting into what you consider your physical world, but it is an illusion. It is not real. Your real self is safe, connected to Source, connected to All That Is, connected to God.

You Created Your World

There is an aspect of you that has created an illusion in which to experience your beliefs. You are given the creative force of God, the creative force of mind that is all-powerful, and you can bring into manifestation everything you wish to experience. You are given that freedom. Yet deep in the dark realms of your mind, you have this misunderstanding that you have separated yourself from God, from your true nature. You have become frightened, you have become small, and you have become manifested in your physical body. This is what you are experiencing in your world at this moment.

This seems to be an elaborate tale that you cannot believe, for you look around and see what you think is an objective world. You touch your body and think it is real. You see your family and friends as solid and true in the only sense that you understand, but the biggest aspect of your self is not physical. Not until you truly come to understand this fall from grace — that it was merely a mistaken idea that was so powerful in its origins, in the force behind it — will you understand that you created a world to house this idea of untruth, and that is your world. This is why your world is so dangerous. This is why your world is apparently full of death, war, divorce, judgment, and hatred.

When you look around this world in your darkest moments, you ask, "If there is indeed a God, how can this world be created as it is? How can this body in which I live be so faulty and falling apart? How can it be sick with cancer? How can it be ugly? How can it be all these things?" Understand that the one you call God did not create this world, for there is no one God. There is only a benevolent force that permeates all things.

You have been given the ability to experience everything contained within you, and in this moment of your incarnation in what you think is a physical body, you are indeed experiencing that which is untrue. This is the world you find yourself in. This is blasphemy to those who believe God created this world. God did not create it. However, it is influenced by God when you raise your self out of the physical and go inside to connect with the spiritual, when you begin to comprehend what has happened and who you are. Then you can reach up toward the light to connect with higher realms, vibrations, and higher energies. Things begin to shift for you, not because you are being rewarded from a divine being who is patting you on the head and saying, "Well done! You have recognized that I am God," but because you recognize the truth — that you are living in a world of untruth, difficulty, separation, scarcity, and disease.

When you begin to realize the truth, you raise your mind from the lie that you are living. Your world begins to shift not because you are being rewarded but because you are aligning with truth. In totally aligning with truth, you will begin to transform your world. This phrase is the truth: "Be the change you wish to see in the world." This is truth because you create the world from your mind, you create the body from your mind, and you create all that is uncomfortable. All the suffering you experience is from the mind.

Realize the Truth

You cannot understand your experience until you realize that the body is not who you are, and indeed, this world is not who you truly are. Only in comprehending this truth can you view the body differently and begin to understand its function. You learn how to raise your self from the lower vibrations to the higher vibrations to tap into truth. Then your world can reflect truth.

This is the most difficult thing for you to understand, and it is the most frightening aspect of your dream. It seems to make you vulnerable, susceptible to death, and unable to reach your dreams. It seems to make you unable to be who you wish to be. The truth is you are limited when

6 ✳ Spirit of the Western Way

you see yourself as a body. You do not comprehend your true nature when you focus on the body.

In the Western world, the body has become a god. The body has become the definer of what and who you are. You see your value represented in your body's shape and size, the clothes you put on it, the jewelry you wear, and the style of your hair. You define yourself by the sicknesses you fear, the weaknesses that permeate your body, and the aging you endure. You do not seem to have any control over it. You see it as something that is fallible, judged and judgmental all at the same time. So here we begin our story of opening the door to freedom. Entertain this idea, and understand that the body is not who you are. Plant that seed now.

Imagine a corpse, a body that has lost its spirit. It is not beautiful. It cannot do anything, and it has no volition of its own. It is animated only by your spirit, by your force of being, and it is this realization that is necessary for you to transform your relationship with your body. You ask your body to do everything it does. Your ideas, beliefs, values, actions, words, and feelings infiltrate the body. Of itself, the body does nothing. It is as a corpse, and it is only through your divine being, through your divine nature, that it does anything at all. Again, imagine a corpse, a body devoid of life that does not pulse with passion or breath or color or joy. It lies there empty. That is what the body is; it is nothing more. The life that you feel in your body — the energy that you feel in your fingertips, in your heart, in your mind, in your toes, in your belly — that is all you. That is the real you, the energy of you. That is what you are! This is the focus we ask you to take.

> Sit quietly for a few moments and feel the life force in your body. Go from the top of your head down through your face, through your throat, and down to your fingertips. Go down through your chest, your belly, your hips, your sexual organs, your legs, your feet, and every part of you. Feel the life force throbbing in your body.

It is not the body that makes this energy; it is you! It is your spirit, your mind, and your soul expressing through the physical. It is only in this realization that you will come to see you can transform the body, heal the body, and make the body behave in a way that is in alignment.

The Dream

The body is, indeed, a manufactured aspect of your dream, and as we have said, your idea of your reality is very off-kilter, so to speak. This is the phrase, is it not? Your belief about the body as the most tangible aspect of you is one of the inversions that must happen in your thinking for you to truly grasp what is going on in your experiential world. All the material and information you take in from your experiential world is apparently through the body. So you think you hear things, see things, and taste things, but what is actually happening is you create a feedback system that verifies that which is already verified.

In your mind's eye, you have created a world. You have created an experience that you project outward, re-experiencing it and believing it is new. This is very difficult for the Western mind to understand. It is a sophisticated concept of apparent illogical deception. However, think about your sleeping dream state and the dreams you experience within that realm: You see, taste, talk, fly, and even think you might die. You see faces you think you understand and recognize, and you see unfamiliar faces. These are all experiences that you have within your dream state. It is clear you do not see these things with your physical eyes or touch them with your physical hands, for you are asleep, tucked very nicely in your bed, sawing logs, as you say.

This is evidence that there is some other aspect of the mind that you are not aware of, and this is also what happens in what you consider to be your real world. From our point of view, you are dreaming. There are levels of dreaming, and there are levels of waking. Understand that for many of you, your three-dimensional life that you call your existence is just another level of sleeping.

Take a leap of faith here on this journey with us. Set aside your judgments for a little while so that we can explain what is happening. The

8 ✳ Spirit of the Western Way

experiences you have in the dream state prove that your mental structures are not as you think. You are taught that you see through your eyes, speak with your tongue, and hear through your ears. Yet in your dream state, this is not true, so you have evidence that there is something else going on. Take that aside for the moment, and put it somewhere.

The Warped Feedback System

The reality you experience through your body might not be as real as you think. You have very real, visceral experiences that bring you fear, joy, sexual arousal, and all kinds of things, yet your body is not involved in this; it is only your mind. Think a moment about this concept, and bring it into another level of expression: You are still dreaming when you are in what you consider to be your three-dimensional world.

What you have in front of you as a projection are all the things that have caused your fear, distress, and separation from that which you call God. These are the mistaken ideas and beliefs of the mind. When you project them into the apparent separate world you believe you created, this is what you see as your physical experience. Your body is another projection. It is not real in the sense you believe it is real. It is your belief in your isolation manifested into an illusion of that experience.

So your body is a physical manifestation of your belief in separation. This seems like an unusual concept, but stay with us. Put aside your judgments and what you have learned, for what you have been taught causes your suffering. Your misunderstandings cause your fears and lack of abundance and poor health. This is why we must come at this subject from the most basic principles, for if you continue to believe in what you have believed in, you cannot make any substantial changes in your experience. You will re-experience that which you believe to be true, and if that is out of alignment with truth, which a lot of what you believe is, you will live in a difficult world. This is why you perpetually have physical issues. You feel separated, fearful, and isolated because you believe in untruth. We must tackle this from the most foundational beliefs you have; otherwise, we cannot deal with the effects of your belief system. If we begin where you are standing, which is looking at the world as a reality, as something that is objective and happening to you without any affect from you, then we can see you are imprisoned in the mind of untruth, and we wish to free you from it.

This is why the world of your projected fears, beliefs, and misunderstandings that you live in is so distressing to you. There is an aspect of you too that is manifesting the body. Now, this aspect of you that manifests the body is your desire for individuality, your desire for control and creative superiority — imperialism, we would say. You believe you are the creator of all your experiences and you are in control of everything, and if you do not wield this control, everything will fall apart. What you must understand is that your body is a manifestation of these ideas and is used as evidence to support that which you believe in.

This is a warped feedback system. You picked the very thing you created to collect evidence to prove that the thing you created is real. So here you are. You have created a body to reinforce your sense of separation, and you use the body to collect information to prove that you are separate. This is why it is such a difficult concept to understand. You feed yourself information all the time that reinforces your beliefs about what you have become, and you tell yourself lies. You are not separate from that which you call God, that which you call love; you only believe you are. Your mind is so powerful and creative that you have created a world that is evidence of your misbelief, and your body is part and parcel of that evidence you create for yourself.

It is a very sophisticated concept that this is not the world you live in according to your teachings, and this is why you suffer. This is why you are fearful and terrified by love and why you become sick. You believe in untruths, and you reinforce them all the time, not understanding that this is what you do.

We refer back to the body. You have a vehicle that seeks information through sight, sound, taste, and experience to reinforce the beliefs you feel you need to be safe within this separated world you created. This is what the teachings were in the book you call the New Testament. This is what the one you call Jesus was trying to teach you. Understand that there have been attempts to convey this information before and many since, but this is the one we address here, for it is important in your culture. The teachings that this being brought through his enlightenment and experiences have been misunderstood. Your Judeo-Christian culture and the misunderstandings it is founded on are part and parcel of this text and teaching.

You will find that there are many teachings in your mind that reinforce your misperceptions, and they seem to come from places of authority: the church, science, teachers, and parents. We will crack the veneer of your civilization in a way, and we will come at the body from a completely different point of view. This might cause you some distress, some discomfort, for we say things that are very difficult for you to believe, given the massive amount of evidence you bring to yourself that contradicts what we say.

Your mind believes in the movie it is watching, just as when you go to a movie theater. You become involved in the emotions of the characters and you believe the story, yet it is nothing more substantial than a light shining on a screen, flickering and creating images you believe in. This is exactly what happens in your mind, and again we ask you to recall a corpse. This is what your body truly is. It is nothing! All the animation, all the ideas, and all the experiences come from the force that is the mind, and you put them into the body. You put your prejudices and your fears into your body. You put your pleasures and delight into your body. You put your value system into your body. This is what animates it and causes your behavior.

Your behavior does not arise from anything other than your beliefs and understandings of what you are and how things function. We are building on the true description of what motivates you, the true description of what happens in (what you call) your physicality and within your perception. You cannot separate your body from your perception because your perception creates your body.

You must understand that those of us in the nonphysical, those of us who are not incarnated, come to your awareness with an awakened mind. We can see your errors and misunderstandings, and we can assist you by shining a light on those areas of darkness and misperception that you still believe. It is similar to waking a child from a nightmare: You come into the room and find the child screaming and fearful, seeing a world you know is not real, and you must wake that child. That is what we are doing with you, and we use the word "child" not in condescension but as a description of innocence and inexperience. You are early in your waking journeys, so what we say seems foreign and unreliable and questionable.

There is much in your mind, even as you read this, that will prompt you to think, "This cannot be true, for my world feels real and my experiences feel real." And it is real for you, dear ones. This is the paradox. As long as you believe in the dream, you are immersed in its story, you are immersed in its emotions, and you are immersed in its suffering. We are trying to wake you from a nightmare and into a pleasant dream. However, the body is deeply involved in the dream, and we discuss that more later on. For now, sit with this information we have given you. Sit with this information that the body is your own creation to reinforce your sense of separation and that this is why it causes such difficulty and such pain. When you focus on the body, believing that it is what you are, you reinforce your feelings of separation and isolation.

In your culture, your materialistic and secular belief that you are only a body having a completely physical experience causes many of you to not believe in the nonphysical in any way at all. You dismiss dreams, emotions, and energies, and you are deeply immersed in believing the body, believing the evidence of the body. You suffer deeply because this is a symbol of isolation and separation, and the more you believe in it, the more profoundly you focus on it to bring that which you wish for to your experience. The more lost in the darkness you are, the more distance there is between you and truth, so your suffering increases.

This is something you see, for example, in eating disorders and other body-obsession disorders. In that situation, a being is so immersed in the physicality of who he or she is and what is valuable about that person's body that he or she becomes completely disconnected from reality. The body becomes a god in all ways. The person desperately tries to make things happen through the body, but it is impossible. The body does not make anything happen. The body is an effect, not a cause, and when you identify with it as the cause of things, you are lost from truth. You will suffer — not as punishment, but as an indicator from your higher self, from the guidance system you are born with, that you are off track.

CHAPTER 2

The Split Mind Cannot See Truth

You have created this world from the depths of your mind, and you have packaged all the untruths about yourself within your body. So you can see how this is a setup for disaster. You have manufactured a world to show you your shortcomings, and it is not because you are stupid (although it sounds quite ridiculous when you word it this way). What you are doing is using your creative nature, for as a divine being, you are creative in all aspects. You have the opportunity to create in alignment with truth, or you have the opportunity to make out of alignment with lies. Your purpose is to create or to make.

When you make things, you make them from a sense of misinterpretation. You make them from your confusion and misunderstandings. When you create in alignment with truth, your mind is clarified because you have identified with what is true reality, not your fictitious reality. When this happens, the mind shifts and becomes integrated, or whole. It becomes aligned with the vibration of love, which is the vibration of what you call God, what you call divine creativity. When you are in alignment with that, all things go well, your experience on this planet shifts, and you eventually no longer have to be born in a body. This is what you call enlightenment, but we will not go into that now, for you are not there yet.

You are reading this book in your physical body in your physical world. You believe in your physical world, so we are speaking about the

14 ✴ Spirit of the Western Way

making rather than the creating. Now, these words are used interchangeably in your society, but pay particular attention to them. When you make something, you are out of alignment with truth; when you create, you are in alignment with truth. This is something to remember because these are not definitions you use. "Creating" and "making" are often used in the same way, but we are being quite specific. We use those words according to our definition so that you do not get confused.

Western Society Is Founded on Misteachings

When you are in a sleeping state and do not realize the dream you live in is your own creation and the body you are in is your personally manufactured symbol of separation, this is where suffering arises, for you are not in alignment with truth. Your mind is fractured in the sense that you project outside your mind everything that is not true, so you see your fears appear in the world. You see conflicts in the world and in your relationships. You see "the other" as guilty, for you project your fears and hidden ideas of guilt into the world after your separation from All That Is. You cannot live with this kind of conflict and fear that has arisen in the mind because of the separation from All That Is. Now you understand this, and you feel separate. It is your experience, but it is not the truth.

All the great teachings of the world point to experiences had by those who transcribed the material or who had that spiritual experience. They tried to explain what it is like to be connected to All That Is, what it is like to understand the reality of your true nature, but this is an experience that is very, very difficult to explain. These great teachers from the past used words that ordinary beings might understand, but of course, there is no language to define the divine experience of revelation or direct contact with All That Is. Such words are not in your repertoire. They are words that are not defined in your culture, so the beings who have had this experience struggle to explain it, and unfortunately, the split mind of the ordinary human being who has not had this transcendental experience does not understand what it is talking about and makes up stories.

This is the experience you have had in your culture with the one known as Jesus, the one who we are, in fact, working in concert with. Do not throw the book across the room because we say this. Understand that he was a being who was merely having this experience of creation, this revelatory connection with All That Is, and he tried to explain it to people who were deeply immersed in the material world. This is where the foundation of his teachings — his awakening, his connection to creation — arose from, but the language he had to communicate these massive concepts was narrow, and the concepts had to be simplified so that the beings he communed with stood a chance of understanding them.

We will not go into that in depth here; we are merely pointing out the cause of confusion around this being's teachings because your society's value system is based on his teachings. Even if you are not a Christian, someone who does not go to church or who thinks the stories of Jesus Christ and the Bible are fabricated, your society is nonetheless built on them. Your laws are based on them. Your definitions of right and wrong are based on them. Your understanding of what is good, what is achievable, and what is desirable are based on them. So even if you are an atheist, someone who hates religion or simply Christianity, or someone who does not agree about the definition of the one called Jesus, understand that we are here to assist in deconstructing your conditioned mind pertaining to these teachings.

Bear with us not because we are preaching Christianity — oh no, we are not doing that! We are giving you an understanding of your society's definition of things, and we are still working on the body. We must digress occasionally into the structures that your society has made out of misunderstanding. Many of the Christian beliefs interwoven within your cultural institutions are incorrect, and they are based on the split mind, the divided mind, the confused mind, and the mind that incorrectly interpreted divine doctrine. We are deconstructing your social conditioning, and we wish to plant the seed that your society is based on many untruths.

When the mind is split, it does not understand how it was created or what it is doing, and the world becomes its enemy. The body also becomes its enemy. It does not identify with the body as something that can be its ally because it is confused in its value system. It will attack the body for being fallible. It will hate the body for not providing it with that which it wants. It will deny the body its simple experience, for it will have value judgments about it that are out of accord with truth, and it will project into the world all the judgment and guilt it tries to avoid within itself.

16 ✳ Spirit of the Western Way

Understand that you have created the world and the body to relieve you from the suffering of guilt and fear. You have created a place to put your guilt and fear, and it is in the outside world, in those enemies and people you love to judge and gossip about, and you have also put it in your body. You have a perception of the body that can be either quite hateful, in the sense that you will abuse it and cause it pain through unhealthy habits, or worshipful, in the sense that you think it is your salvation and it will bring you everything you want. You do not have a real comprehension of your spiritual nature, so you turn to what you believe in, which is the physical world. You turn to the material: money and bodies — not only your body, but also other beings' bodies in the hopes that they can give you what you want.

You can indeed envision your society worshiping the body through extreme exercise, through the adornment of it with makeup and hairstyles. You can see the worshiping of the body through raiment as people endlessly buy clothes to make themselves feel worthy and happy and beautiful. You can see that there is an obsession with food in your society, which is a way of numbing the body's discord. You feel discord and blame it on the body. Consuming food temporarily soothes these discordant feelings, but those feelings are really ideas — they are not physical — and the stimulation of the physical senses distracts you for a little while so that you feel relief. So we will go into each of these subjects in detail, and we will explain what is happening. We will explain what the mind does and how it uses the body as a source of relief from mental anguish.

Higher Mind and Ego Mind

Let us define the ego mind so that you are under no illusions. In your ordinary culture, you think of the ego as that brash and loud part of you that shows off and is very happy to talk about itself. You say that someone who is arrogant or self-aggrandizing has a big ego, but in this text, we use the term "ego mind" in a different way. In your society, you think your brain creates your thoughts, your ideas, and your personality. As a secular society, you are repeatedly taught that thoughts arise from electrical circuits within the brain. This is not the case. You are indeed walking around in a giant receiver of information and ideas that come through the body from the nonphysical. You literally are receiving information.

All your thoughts and ideas are not contained within the structure of the brain as you have been taught; they have been translated by the brain, and the information comes through in the form of concepts actually being transmitted by the universal mind. The ego mind is what you might consider a lower-vibration transmitting station. It contains all the negative and fearful low-vibration thoughts that have ever been thought. It is as if you are tuning into a dark and negative radio station that only talks about hateful things.

The higher mind — the universal mind, the mind of God, if you will — the consciousness that we reside in, is another station you can tune into. In that station, you can tune into inspiring ideas; motivations to do good works; peaceful, contemplative music; and other wonderful things that enliven your life and bring you information that is required for sound decision making and all sorts of wonderful and delicious gifts.

Misunderstanding acts out within your mind every day. You think that, in some way, your self generates the stream of thoughts that goes through your head. This is not the case. The things you repeatedly focus on, ingest, and speak about create the vibration you function at. It's not so much that which you do — despite the obvious dark and devious things. These behaviors arise from thought, so we say that thoughts are more powerful than action in this sense. You do not rob someone's house unless you have had thousands of thoughts of scarcity, poverty, and lack of abundance. Your behavior is the last result, so to speak.

So you have this transponder, this receiver, picking up information, and you think it is your own. You think the ideas are yours. You are working under a misconception here. Ego mind is not yours alone; it is a shared conglomeration of negativities, a shared cultural conglomeration of false ideas, narrowness, darkness, and unloving concepts. When you focus on judgment — let us say when you focus on your body, for this is one of the large triggers that forces you to delve into the ego mind vibration — you begin to receive these concepts. If these ideas are about scarcity, they will make you think that there will be a change at your work and you will be fired.

These ideas in the ego mind are about ugliness and judgment of the body; therefore, you look in the mirror, and if you tune into the ego mind through your focus, you see your body as ugly. You see your shape as

18 ✳ Spirit of the Western Way

unattractive, and you tell yourself stories of being unlovable. As you believe these thoughts, your vibration lowers, and you pick up a momentum that continues to tune you into this radio station of the ego mind. You have more and more and more negative, hateful, and judgmental thoughts that become self-fulfilling prophecies, and these pick up momentum just as a snowball rolling down a hill picks up more and more snow. This thing becomes very difficult to stop. This is what the ego mind is.

Now, the higher mind is also similar to a radio station that can tune into a very clear signal, and this is what we are about. We are about teaching you how to tune into and focus on the higher mind. It is a process of undoing, for you have been trained in this world to focus on the ego mind. It is a tricky job for us to stop the momentum, for much of the momentum of your mind says that what we speak about here is untrue because it does not align with the station you tune into.

In regard to the body, we wish you to view it through the higher mind, for you are indeed ensconced within its limitations for a time while you journey on this plane. It is very important for you to understand these two different minds that are not contained within your body. This is a teaching mistake of your culture. If you function under this mistaken belief that your thoughts are yours alone and they arise of their own volition and should be believed, you are focusing on the body from the ego mind, and you will go into fear. You will go into narrowness of thought, judgment, and self-loathing. When you tune into the ego mind, you attack the body.

The ego, in its grandiosity, in its belief that it knows everything (for it is not a modest or sane state of mind to be in), is inconsistent because it is full of hatred, which is the opposite of what you are. It is full of lies and deceits and untruths, and it has lots of evidence to prove its case. This is the confusing part for those of you who are new to venturing in this realm. You look around at the world and see reasons for judgment. You look around at the world and see reasons for fear. You look around at the world and see reasons to purchase a gun to defend yourself against negativity. If you do not understand that you are picking up on all the negative concepts and ideas that have ever been thought, you think that these fears are real, and you believe that you will not be safe, your body will not be safe. We emphasize this, for all of the ego's thoughts are about improving the body, attacking the body, judging the body, and lusting after bodies. These kinds of concepts that are contained within the ego mind make you feel frightened and needy, and they constantly lower your vibration. It is a place of destruction and of hellish consciousness.

This is what deep and dark depression is: a mind immersed in the ego (by our definition, not by your normal definition of ego). When this momentum picks up, when this dark and dirty "snowball" picks up energy, you attract more and more negative thoughts, and because of your mistaken teachings about the mind, you do not know to not listen to them. You do not know that you have the ability to train the mind to focus on that which you wish for.

Our definition of higher mind is the collection of thoughts that are high and loving in nature and are nonjudgmental, compassionate, creative, and appreciative of yourself and others. These concepts are contained within the transmissions of higher mind, but if you do not understand you are the focusing device and do not know you are the one in control of what you receive, you have difficulty tapping into this higher mind because of the culture in which you live and particularly because of your culture's focus on the body. As we have said, when you believe in the body — when you love or lust after the body and believe that it will bring you that which you need — then you are in the ego mind, the lower mind that is associated with all of these other thoughts and negativities, and you will not be able to reach the higher mind.

The higher mind — the spiritual realms, the divine realms, or the realms of miracles — is not physical and is not associated with the physical material world. We must teach you how to focus on the higher mind and that the body is one of the triggers when you believe it exists in the way the Western mind does. The body takes you down to the ego mind, and there you become lost, frightened, and even more contaminated with ideas that are not in your best interest. So those are the ego mind and the higher mind. We will refer to these two levels of mind quite frequently, so be sure you understand them.

As you travel through your day today, we would like you to look at your thoughts in a different way. Look at your thoughts to see whether you can discern which part of the mind they are coming from. Are they coming from the ego mind or the higher mind? Do you look at a flower in your garden with appreciation and joyous in its beauty and perfection? Or do you look at your lawn and wish you didn't have to mow it and hate the dandelions in it? These are two thoughts that could stream across the mind, and you immediately know which is which. One will take you further into darkness, and one will lift you into the realms of love.

Put the book down for a little while, and pay attention to the thoughts in your mind. You will begin to understand where you are. You will begin to understand what is happening. If your thoughts venture toward the body's weaknesses or lack of security, then you can be sure you are in the ego mind, and you are in treacherous waters. You are in a bog that is laced with hidden quicksand and sticky mud that will make your journey difficult.

CHAPTER 3

Break Free from Your Prison

You created the body from your beliefs. When you have a body, your beliefs literally tell you, through the creation of the body, that you believe in separation, that you believe in your lack of connection to God, to Spirit. That is why you are born in a body. You believe in its individuality, in its fallibility — in the world, so to speak. That is why you are here and in a body.

When you come into this world, you believe in it to some degree. You believe in your ability to make whatever you choose in the sanctity of your self (we say this with a small *s*), but this very thing is what creates sickness because the body, in and of itself, is fallible and a representation of the mistakes of the mind. So you can see that the deck is stacked against you from the beginning. Understand that the realization of Oneness and your focus on spiritual matters shift your energies around the body because they shift your beliefs about the body.

You come into this life with many negative beliefs about yourself, the body, death, and so on. You are further conditioned by the manifestation of these beliefs in outward experiences, such as relationships, occurrences, ideas, and education. They reinforce your belief in that which you have in your mind. Now this cycle seems as if it would be impossible to break, for if you always bring to you that which you believe in and collect evidence that it is true, how can you break it? You are in a maze of thought that constantly reinforces itself. How do you break out of it?

There comes a point when you have suffered enough, and you all suffer in this world; that is a truth of your experience here. In your ordinary mind, your ordinary day, and your ordinary life, you suffer. There are things that go wrong or that you feel are not right. There are things you observe that cause pain. There are internal processes — headaches, stomachaches, broken bones, accidents, and strange and random events that cause difficulty in life. You experience this through the body, but what you must understand is that all these things go together. Your belief in the body, your belief in the world, and your belief in separation manifest back through your mind and through your experiences, creating a never-ending loop of evidence that proves that which you believe to be true.

When you get sick of this, you will realize that there must be a better way, for there cannot be any truth to what you experience because an aspect of your mind knows that there is a nonphysical element to this experience. There is an aspect of the mind that is still connected to Oneness, that which you call God.

That Oneness, that connection, speaks to you in whispers at first, it is true, because your belief in the world and in the body is powerful. Your indoctrination in these untruths is extreme and repetitive and consuming, yet a voice remains there: "This cannot be all there is. This cannot be all there is." When you have suffered enough and you realize that all of the things you pursue — relationships, food, sex, money — have been pursued to your heart's desire, then an aspect of you realizes these things do not bring you what you seek.

You seek outside yourself because you have been told you are a material body. You have been told that it is the material that will satisfy you, and that is not true, for you are not a material being. This is a terrible error, and it is only through intense suffering, initially, that you begin to realize there must be another way. And there are beings on your plane who are more evolved than you and have higher consciousness, and they are here to teach you. You can always look to other beings to see whether they are happier than you. You can always look to other beings to see whether they are healthier than you. You know there must be another way, another experience to be had. These are the small cracks that begin to appear in the conditioned mind.

Some of you try to patch these cracks by medicating because you are fearful. You fear that you will not be able to continue your responsibilities. You fear that you are losing touch with reality, and you wish to make a run for it. You wish to leave because you know that the life you have started and that you are experiencing is not what you want, and it is not making you happy. But because of your conditioning, there are many people, places, and things — careers, mortgages, children, or spouses — that depend on you in this life that you find yourself in. This is what you consider the midlife crisis. This describes the person who is about to have a nervous breakdown.

Of course on Spirit's side, this is applauded and considered most precious, but in your society and in the conditioning you have there, this is not considered good. You are asked to stay the same, to choose careers and partners for life. You are asked to override your feelings and to hide your emotions. Many things in your culture force you into not following your heart's desire, and your heart's desire is your spirit speaking.

Some of you rebel at a young age and become artists or philosophers or musicians, following a path of passion and extreme experience. This is true, but the vast majority of you are not really living lives you consider authentic or passionate. You have done as you were taught, and you have been taught because of what you believe. This has reinforced what you already held within the mind that you were born with.

Here you are, small cracks appearing in your façade, the social face you present to the world. And it is here that you have the opportunity to open, grow, and enter into a real life, an authentic life. For so many of you, the conditioned mind overrules everything. The family, the culture, and the religion you were born into (through your own volition, of course) represent your belief system, so you cannot blame it for where you are; it is your own creation. Initially, it felt like a comfortable shoe because it was what you believed in, what you wanted before you were born, but there is also wisdom hidden within the higher mind that speaks to you of your true nature, your true self. That voice becomes louder as you get older. This world is designed to show you the inconsistencies and fractured weaknesses of your beliefs so that they do not last. You will become disillusioned with them.

24 ✳ Spirit of the Western Way

Understand that you may have had many, many lives of believing in, experiencing, and feeling that your dreams still have something to offer you, but eventually (and this is happening for many of you on this plane now), you experience disillusionment. You look around at how you live, what you buy, and what you consume, and you feel a deep, nagging discontent. This is Spirit knocking on your door. Many of you will not open the door, for you are scared of the stranger there, what you'll be asked and whether you'll invite Spirit in and begin to change things. You know deep inside that the knock at the door will shake things up, so you refuse to answer.

You repress creative energies that wish to be expressed. You repress passion. You might desire to travel, but you do not travel. You might desire to paint, but you do not paint. Instead, you vacuum and do dishes to maintain a façade of social acceptance. You might wish to garden in a warm climate, yet you live in a cold one. There are many things that we can bring to mind, but you know what it is for you at this time.

Perhaps you have committed to a relationship that you no longer want, and you are terrified of the consequences of walking out the door and saying "Thank you. I am done here. I wish you well, but I am leaving." These are all things that run through your mind when you work with this material. Listen to these voices. They are the voices of your true self — the voices of your natural self — speaking, clawing, and trying to be heard over the conditioning you have been through.

You now wonder, "How can our society continue if we behave in this way? How can we continue on in civilization if we listen to these voices? Surely all will crumble. Surely all will fall apart, and we will be a society of anarchists and rebels and street people."

Look around at your society. Take a good, honest look as objectively as you can at what is happening. You have a society of fractured relationships. You have a society of unconscious addiction to many different things. You have a society that is destroying the most beautiful planet. It's a rich planet full of life and glorious experiences with different climates, vegetation, animals, and birds, but you sit in boxes and watch boxes, feeling sad about going to work or about being unable to make love to your partner. You scream at your children and tune out from anything that is real, anything that is of value. You ignore your creativity and wish you were somewhere else living another life.

Your Body Doesn't Limit You

What would happen if you were to follow your heart? What would happen if you were to follow your dreams? What would happen if you were to open your mind to the limitless possibilities of love and creativity and communion? We think the world you would create would be much better, and you would see that many of the sicknesses you suffer from are not the body's fault but the mind's. They are the mind expressing its energies, its desire for creativity, freedom, and love. The sicknesses you suffer repress those energies. You stuff them down with food, drugs, and alcohol. You stuff them down with endless hours of television and a constant barrage of hateful comments in the mind that tell it to shut up, be quiet, behave, and do as it is told. The conditioned aspects of your mind become the prison keepers. It is a vicious cycle.

Begin to listen to those voices. You do not have to destroy your life as you know it, but if you wish to be healthy, if you want your arthritis and ulcers and heart attacks to go away, understand that the body reflects the mind. Understand that all sicknesses that manifest in your physical structure are blocks to the energy that is naturally designed to flow through you: creativity, openness, love, communion, compassion, connection, foolishness, humor, playfulness, and sexual activity. These are all in your natural state, and when you look at them from your conditioned mind's state, you cannot imagine what a life of experiencing these things would be like. It looks very different from the mortgage, the job, the acquisition of possessions, and the restrictions that you feel make up your life. You perceive that the body limits you.

Your body is not limiting you; your mind is limiting you, and your body simply represents your mind. It is a physical manifestation of all that goes on inside your mind. So here we have the issue of your sicknesses, your high blood pressure, your gnarled and rigid limbs, and your closed heart manifesting as a heart problem. These are all physical, energetic manifestations of ideas and beliefs that are not in alignment with truth. When your mind is aligned with truth, your body functions in a beautiful way, representing that which you are. Understand that your negative health issues are gifts from the universe. They are not curses from a badly organized God; they are gifts from the universe, this one that you might call God, this benevolent force that is always pushing you toward love.

Sicknesses are messages from love that you are not in accord with it; you are out of alignment with it. Illness shows you what is going on by its location in your body. Its location in your energetic system shows you what it is you are up to. See the problems in your life as treasure maps that show you where to find what is amiss in your mind. This is what the world is: a physical manifestation of that which is untrue in your mind. It is also a physical manifestation of that which is true in the mind, but as long as you have untruth, you will be born into this physical three-dimensional world. When all untruths are gone and you are at complete peace, complete communion with love, you will no longer need to manifest here to experience, see, and feel that which is untrue about yourself. Now you are ensconced in this illusion, which is a demonstration of what you are.

Think about this: What is your body saying? What part of your body hurts? What part of your body is not functioning at peak capacity? What part of your body is unloved by your mind? By embracing the unloving condemnation of a physical aspect of your body, you bring dysfunction to it! Pay attention to that. When you look at your body with hatred, you bring sickness on it, for the body functions perfectly in a state of love, acceptance, compassion, forgiveness, joy, creativity, and connection. When you restrict the flow of love, the flow of this natural true self, then it manifests in the body as restriction, disease, and mental or emotional dysfunction.

You call these things sicknesses and diseases in your society, but they are not. When you call them sicknesses, you say they are things that arise of their own volition. They do not. They arise from a million thoughts in your mind. They arise from a million hateful ideas, from fears, and from judgments. These manifest in the body (not only in the body, and that's what we are speaking about now). You will learn some ways to unravel the mystery of sickness and the apparent fallibility of the body.

CHAPTER 4

Understand Your Chakras

Different areas of your body relate to different emotions and aspects of your self, your life, and your being. We will now discuss the chakra system, which is often described in Eastern philosophies and is creeping into the Western mind through yoga and New Age practices. We introduce it here as truth of its existence. It is indeed a verifiable system of energies that creates your body.

There are thirteen chakras (Western minds are often only familiar with seven), some of which reside outside the body and relate to the nonphysical. The ones you are aware of in the Western world through the esoteric teachings of the yogic practices relate to different areas of the body, and they are responsible for the production of the physical manifestation of certain areas of the body. Remember, the body represents the mind. If the body represents aspects of the mind, then your physical body will manifest, through thought, those aspects of the mind that relate to certain areas. Each focal point of the chakra system is responsible for creating a certain area of the body, and each point in the chakra system has particular aspects of mind flowing through it and manifesting in it.

Let's start at the base chakra. The base chakra is about your beingness on the physical plane — your feeling that you have a right to be here — and pertains to your tribal or family structure. It is located at the base of

27

the spine and is responsible for the sacral region: the back, the hips, the pelvis, the tailbone, and the elimination area of the body.

The second chakra is the sexual energy chakra located just above the first chakra in the gonad region of your sexual reproductive organs. It is responsible for creativity in the physical sense, movement and flexibility, and self-expression through action. It pertains to your children and the physical organs that reside in this area: the sexual organs, the uterus, the testes, the lower abdominal cavity, and the lower areas of digestion.

The third chakra is what you consider the solar plexus and is represented in the physical body with a collection of nerve endings and a focus of physical organ structures. This particular chakra represents your personal power, your ability to change things by exerting physical will over them to make things happen. It is your sense of self in the ego and of physicality in the world. It is your ability to act on that which you wish to do, change, or affect.

These three chakras are in the realm of the ego. They are, indeed, related to the physical body, birth, sexual reproduction, and power. Engaging in physical activity is their purpose, and they are foundational in the sense that they are at the bottom of this "tower of power" we describe.

Now you enter the heart chakra, which represents unconditional love and acceptance and is where massive transformation happens. It represents love of others and of self, including the romantic ideal. It represents the ability of the human to give for no other purpose than to share with someone else, and it is this chakra that represents the heart, the lungs, and the thoracic region. It is here that you transcend the three chakras of the lower realms, the ego and the physical body. It is through the heart chakra that things begin to shift and transform into the higher realms.

You have a physical representation of your world within your body. This is an interesting thing to think about. You have all the aspects of your physical experience represented within your physical, energetic body. Many things are going on here. There are representations of the outer world in your inner self, and there are representations of your inner self in your outer world. Remember, your mind has created all this, so of course there are physiological and physical representations of mental structures that express in the outside world and show up in your physical body. Your body speaks to you about areas of healing and things that need to shift. For example, you might have a fractured relationship with a member of your family, and this might show up as lower back pain at the bottom of the spine where your tribal and family structures are represented.

As we continue up this tower of power (this is a fun and appropriately descriptive name for the chakra system), we enter the throat chakra, which represents self-expression in the higher realms through poetry, speech, and communion. This is where you say who you are. This is where you motivate creation through the spoken word. You must remember that words create. When you say things over and over again, you create them, so this is a very powerful chakra.

If you have confinements within this energy — if you do not speak your mind or if you keep yourself small so that you do not create within the world in this way — you will have problems with your thyroid. This is a common problem in your society, particularly with women because they do not speak up. They do not express themselves honestly and authentically. They are often too busy managing the household's food and chores and doing things for other people. They often do not express themselves as they should and subjugate this aspect of themselves, so they suffer from thyroid problems, for example, that cause weakness and lack of energy. This reinforces their inability to act in the world as individual beings. The mirrored aspect of sickness tells you what is going on. The body is not full enough of energy or itself, so it cannot express itself. Then there is weight gain and lethargy, further diminishing self-expression. It is a self-perpetuating cycle.

We move up to your third eye, which is your psychic development. Now, in your secular society that is so afraid of the nonphysical, many of you have issues in this particular area. Many of you have migraine headaches because you do not use your intuition, you do not interpret your dreams, and you do not meditate. These things balance this particular area of the body and psyche. Headaches, brain tumors, and these kinds of things are caused by a lack of balance within this area.

Monitor Your Energetic Condition

Of course, each chakra can have too much or too little energy going through it, and the sicknesses that show up will represent the energetic condition. So a migraine headache, for example, is a restriction in blood flow to this particular part of the body. This means that you are shutting down your intuitions, these nonphysical contacts that this area of the body-mind complex is in charge of.

Then we move to the crown chakra. This chakra is responsible for your connection to the nonphysical, the Divine, and your connection to that which is out of this world. Examples of physical problems that arise in this area include nightmares and phobias. What you see is a disconnection from Source, so you are deep in fear because you are not connected to God. You become fearful of your existence and the mind, and you lose touch with this area of yourself, your ability to connect with Source, your ability to connect with nonphysical beings such as us.

You have several more chakra centers above the head that relate to other realms, other dimensions, but they are not of any great consequence to us at this point. Once you become an awakened being, these centers become much more important. They are accessible to you when you become a more enlightened being and have your seven physical aspects balanced. You cannot really enter the other realms until you have these seven chakra points balanced and functioning at full capacity.

So your physical structure is divided into areas, and you will find that limited beliefs will manifest as limits in your physical body. Suffice to say, your particular sickness or limitation will manifest in one of the seven chakra areas, and this system gives you a clue as to what is actually going on.

Let's say you have liver cancer. This is in the central part of the body, which is governed by the solar plexus. The liver removes toxins from the body, so you would need to look at your internal pollution. What dirty things are you saying to yourself? We don't mean sexually explicit thoughts; rather, we refer to polluting thoughts. Perhaps you have poisonous ideas about yourself that are manifesting in the liver structure and are growing. Cancer is a disease of overabundance and overproduction. So look at your thoughts. Are your thoughts poisonous about other people? Are you toxic in your relationships? Is there an unhealthy balance in your food consumption?

It is important, especially in the beginning of your journey, to watch what you eat. Your society is full of toxins, and you will find if you have a disease in this part of your body that it is indeed trying to cleanse you of certain things. Do not eliminate the physical world. Do not look only at the mind, for these are all in concert together. Your poisonous thoughts create a poisonous world, and your misunderstanding of nutrition creates a food production methodology that is toxic. Everything is linked. So if you suffer from liver disease, look to the pollution in your food supply and in your mind. Cleanse yourself physically, mentally, and emotionally of poisons. You will immediately know where the poisons are because they are unpleasant-tasting thoughts, ideas, and foods that enter your body.

This applies to each chakra and each area of your body. If an organ is sick, look at the job it does, the responsibilities it has within the physical structure. Western medicine tells you very nicely what each organ does, and you will find that there is a pretty clear and uncomplicated comparison between function and ailment. Investigate this with an open heart and an open mind. It goes against your Western training, but do not let that stop you. Do not let old ideas of physicality stop you. Your body is created by your mind; there are no ifs, ands, or buts about it!

When your body expresses negativity in the sense of a limitation or a disease of some kind, open up your mind to these new ideas. Understand that your body is trying desperately to communicate with you. Listen to it, or you will not fare well. This is not a punishment from a demented god, a judgmental being who has deemed you as bad and therefore must die, for there is no such thing as death as you know it. That is not what this life is for.

This life is for you to learn how you are out of alignment with truth, and if you have manifested a physical illness, there is a message you have sent yourself for many, many years prior to the physical manifestation. When you have a physical manifestation, realize that you have been doing something for a very long time. You have been thinking or feeling something that is out of alignment with truth, so it manifests in the body in an effort to get your attention — to change your mind — so that you can begin to say more loving things and come to a deeper and more loving understanding of what you are and why you are here.

So sickness manifests in the body as the mind produces thoughts, and those thoughts have a certain vibration. To thrive, your body needs to be at the vibration of love, acceptance, and peace. This is its nature. You are designed to live in that space of peace, and when you can access knowledge and understanding from the nonphysical, your life will reflect this in the physical world.

When you are not at peace — when you are in a state of judgment, fear, hatred, or self-loathing — the mind lowers in vibration, and accordingly, the body lowers in vibration, physically manifesting it. You have degrees and different severities of disease. Some are life threatening, and that is because your thoughts and ideas are life threatening. They are full of hate or judgment or self-loathing, whatever the subject.

You can determine the cause when you know where you are limited. If an idea surfaces that you have a particular area of hatred or limitation and you are not happy about it, do not let it form into a physical structure of sickness or disease or a tumor of some kind. Deal with it now. Look at those belief systems that cause pain and suffering, and know that you are not being punished and this is not a dispensation from an angry god. It is a gift from the universe, and it is showing you where you are out of alignment and giving you an opportunity to change the belief system so that you can bring your life into a vibration of love. You can have a happy dream rather than the nightmare you are living.

CHAPTER 5

Nutrition for the Spiritually Minded

Food is the most obvious nutritional device you use in your physical realm — food, water, vitamin supplements, and these kinds of things. Because the body is formed by thought, so too is the nutrition from your food. Now, this is not something you think of when you relate to the physical body because you are convinced that it is a real object, but the truth is your beliefs about food are very limited, which limits and restricts your ability to engage in many other aspects of your consciousness.

You are taught that you must eat a certain quantity of food each day and that it must be of a certain combination of materials (proteins, carbohydrates, fats, and so on). This creates a group consciousness that believes this information. However, such information is not followed around your planet. There are many places where people eat quite differently than you do. They eat vegetarian diets rich in old grains and vegetables, and they manifest a very different energy within the body. Western culture has been greatly affected by the business of food manufacturing. You are, unfortunately, ensconced in a society that has become so far removed from what the human body should be consuming that you have become very confused, very ill, and very heavy in your energies.

Meat and Dairy

Consider the meat production industry in your society. It produces the

33

opposite of what people on spiritual paths should consume. The products are contaminated with chemicals, and pesticides are sprayed on the food fed to those creatures. They are contaminated by fear, for those animals are murdered in a very brutal way, and by medications that they receive. All these impurities enter the body of the creature, and when you ingest it, you ingest those energies. This is when you function in the lower-vibrational realms. There are different reactions to different things as you travel up the vibrational scale. We won't go into the higher realms yet. Let's discuss how you function as a society that consumes these products.

When you function in the ego mind, which most of you do (we do not mean to insult you or tell you that you are unevolved, but most of you believe in the body, which causes you to delve into the ego mind because you really believe in the body, death, and this finite incarnation as the being that you are), then you are at a relatively low vibration on the spiritual scale. This is only an observation from our point of view. We do not wish you to take offense at what we say; we are merely stating what is happening.

You are not at fault here. This is what you are taught in your society: You have a body that is not created by you, and it lives of its own accord with drives and cravings and instincts of its own. These are the misteachings of your society. They are not representative of your intelligence; they have simply been beaten into your mind through the education and conditioning systems that you are victim of in your society.

When you sit down to a steak at dinnertime, you might think you are giving yourself good nutrition. You see it as protein and a source of iron and strength. You do not realize that, in fact, you are keeping yourself out of the realms of higher vibration and poisoning your body with something that is not supposed to be consumed in the form and quantity and manner in which you do it.

The production of meat in your society is not beneficial to raising your vibration because unhealthy and cruel methods are used to raise these animals. They are given an unhealthy diet that passes into their tissues and energetic fields and is then transmitted to you when you consume their bodies.

If you are indeed a carnivore and enjoy eating meat but are curious about raising your vibration and focusing your mind in the higher realms to lift your heavy physical body that is vibrating at the ego's level of oscillation, we suggest you halve the quantity of the meat that you eat and double its quality. If you eat meat every day and purchase it from industrial food production sources, change that to three times a week, and buy organic, locally produced, humanely raised animals.

Now, many arguments might arise in the mind, such as you might have confusion about meals and so forth. You have been raised to believe that protein in this form is required, but it is not. This is a marketing device of food producers who have a tremendous amount of influence and political power, and they lobby to have this misinformation distributed throughout the country. You have been misinformed, and we are here to inform you that even this one step of reducing your commercial meat consumption by 50 percent and replacing it with meat that is humanely raised and humanely killed will provide a tremendous shift in the energies of your body. It is a twofold improvement you will feel. You will feel the lightness from reducing your meat consumption and from reducing the pollution in your body.

Instead of seeing the commercial meat products in your supermarkets as nutritious, see them as contaminating devices that impede your spiritual growth. We would like you to eventually walk past the meat department in your commercial supermarkets and deal with local farmers and butchers. Become very well acquainted with where and how your food is raised. This is the first step in your spiritual journey up the emotional and vibrational scale. You will find that this change alone will reap great benefits.

You also face this misinformation when it comes to your dairy products. These too are produced in a way that is very detrimental to the vibration of the human body. The fat content is too high, and the animals are traumatized. These products result from the destruction of mother-child relationships within the animal kingdom. Think about that! These processes are kept away from you for a purpose. Producers of these products do not want you to see the suffering involved in their production. Milk is a food for youngsters, and in this industry, these poor creatures endure systematic and repeated pregnancies, and their babies are taken away from them violently and without ceremony to produce meat. It is a traumatic and devastating process for the youngsters as well as the mothers.

36　✳　Spirit of the Western Way

When you see dairy products in this way, you will not be able to consume them. It is not possible for you to enjoy a product when you know the suffering it induces in these animals. Now, there are beings who say that milk and dairy products are essential for your structural health. This is not the case at all. This is modern industrial misinformation, or propaganda, that was perpetrated by the producers. Indeed, the consumption of high-fat milk products is detrimental to your body's balance. You are not supposed to eat these products except very occasionally, and they should be organically and locally produced.

There is nothing wrong with eating a piece of organically produced goat cheese or other dairy product, but this should be occasional, what you might consider a treat. It should be something you are aware of doing, something that is honored as a gift given to you by an animal with integrity and its own ability to create. Once again, dairy products should be reduced considerably if not totally removed from your diet. They are not what you are supposed to eat.

The human body is designed to live predominantly on seasonal raw vegetables, nuts, seeds, grains, and fruits. This is the ideal. However, we understand that you live in places where these things are not available or do not grow. The climates you live in are sometimes very cold, and you also have many tropical fruits available to you throughout the year. However, eating locally produced and organic food and less meat and dairy will serve you very well.

Practice Patience in Adjusting Your Diet

When you stuff your body full of too many heavy foods that are contaminated with pesticides and negative energies of fear and distress, all the energy of your body is used to digest the food. The toxins produced from this kind of diet weigh the body down in such a way that there is very little left to play with energetically in the higher realms. There is very little possibility of shifting your consciousness to a higher vibration because digesting this food is such a chore for the physical body. It is very important for spiritual students to understand that diet in the lower realms of vibration is very, very significant.

Now, as you shift to consuming less meat and dairy and more vegetables and opting to switch from chemically drenched foods to organic foods, your body's vibration will rise. You will discover, as you venture into this experiment, that you will easily turn away from things that used to call to you. These are the natural consequences of a vibrational shift. All food has a vibration, and as you shift your consciousness from the body into the higher realms, as you begin to focus on the nonphysical through meditation practice and prayer and relinquish the obsession that the body is your salvation, your vibration will rise. You will tap into higher mind, and you will be naturally inspired to eat a healthier diet.

When you make this decision, it will only be a struggle at first. Your body is acclimated to a certain vibration of food, and it takes several days for it to shift. Understand that this is a vibrational world. Everything has a particular vibration, and you have been functioning at a certain level of thought, action, and food consumption, so we suggest you make a plan of change that takes time. If you eat a conventional Western diet — meat with vegetables and alcohol for dinner, soup and sandwich for lunch, eggs on toast and coffee for breakfast, some unhealthy snacks, and occasionally some deep-fried or fast foods thrown in there — we suggest you take a year to shift from what you are doing to the kind of diet we describe.

The ego mind is a vibrational system that you tap into because of beliefs, conditioning, habits, and availability. There are many reasons you eat the way you do. Many of you do not see your diet as unhealthy; you think it is very healthy because of your conditioning, but in fact, it leads to many diseases. More importantly, it locks you in the physical world, in the material, lower-vibration transmissions of the ego mind, and this is where you suffer.

As you entertain these concepts, understand that this will alleviate your suffering on many levels. When you begin to entertain these changes and you are immersed in an ordinary North American diet, you might feel panicked. That comes from the beliefs you firmly hold about food being challenged by new information. Understand that the stability of your mind and your emotions is predicated on this idea that everything you think is in alignment, that you are not deeply conflicted. As we bring in this new information and you begin to entertain the idea of changing your food, the beliefs you have about the foods you eat will rise to the surface for examination. If you take in the information we bring, there will be conflict with those beliefs.

Have you ever gone on a diet and could not maintain it? Your calm demeanor is based on living in accord with the beliefs you have. We are trying to bring consciousness into your food consumption habits, so we are trying to shift the vibration and behavior into a higher realm. As we introduce these concepts and you start to question what you are doing, your deeply entrenched beliefs rise to the surface. You eat what you eat because you believe in it in some way. You believe that it is nutritious and not harmful. You believe, believe, believe, but this is not necessarily the truth.

You can believe things that are untrue. You believe many things that are not true, and you believe in many things that are, in fact, harming you and preventing you from venturing into the higher realms of Spirit where you will suffer less and have better health and where you will access qualities and abilities that you have no idea you possess.

Eat Natural Foods

Nutrition is not restricted to food. Think of nutrition in all its aspects: body, mind, spirit, heart, soul, and intellect, all the aspects of yourself. There are many aspects to your mind and to your personality, so it is very important that we cover all these things and get you to understand the implications and interrelatedness of them.

Nutrition is derived from many things, but we continue on with food, for it is a many-faceted aspect of nutrition. We do not wish to belabor it, but we go into a few more areas so that you can have some clarity about what is happening with your food intake and what is amiss if you struggle with the quality of your food.

We have said that you are designed to eat a naturally occurring organic diet of vegetables, fruits, nuts, seeds, and grains in their most unprocessed forms. This is your natural state of being. Remember, in your evolutionary history, you have tens of thousands of years of eating food that is unprocessed and unpolluted. Your planet was pristine for much of her life. It is only since the industrial revolution that you began to infiltrate her structure with detrimental, human-made chemical pollution in horrific quantities. In some ways, you have done a tremendous amount of damage. It has reached a level that cannot be ignored as you consider this idea of nutrition.

Nutrition for the Spiritually Minded ✳ 39

A food revolution needs to take place on your planet because you are killing yourselves inadvertently. Your bodies are sending messages to you that are unequivocal to cries for help. Many of you are developing allergies and gastrointestinal problems related to the food industry in North America and elsewhere. North Americans are affecting the entire planet because they consume so many goods that many other countries have fallen victim to the same pesticide-focused and other objectionable food-production methods.

Food must be living to give you life. This is a simple and logical idea. There are several foods in their naturally occurring state — unprocessed nuts, seeds, and grains — that are designed to store food energy for an extended period. If something can be dried and does not mold, then it is designed for this purpose. If it can be stored in a jar on your kitchen shelf for some time in its natural state without rotting, then it is designed for this process. There is nothing wrong with keeping nuts in the fridge to extend their life, but their natural state is to be preserved. You can tell this by the form in which they appear. Dried fruits are another example of this. You can dry grapes and create raisins, and they can sit in a jar on your shelf for some time. They shouldn't be there for years, but they can be there for weeks without any issue at all.

There are many foods in your kitchen and in your cupboards that bear no resemblance to food in its natural state. There are boxes of crackers, cans of processed foods, pizzas, and many other things that have become normal in your paradigm. You see them as food, but they are not really. They do not occur in this state in nature. In fact, there is very little in them that can be recognized as naturally grown. These kinds of foods are detrimental to the body. They contain combinations of preservatives — salts, sugars, and so on — that tantalize your palate, and they are kept in a way that prevents natural oxidation. Foods are meant to be eaten fresh. Drying or keeping a food in a jar in its natural state is the extent of preservation that should be taken.

There are, of course, emergencies when canned foods are perhaps okay, but these items do not give you what your body requires. Your body is designed to be a foraging, naturally harvesting creature. Now, we understand that as you read this and think about your freezers and refrigerators and cupboards full of packaged goods, you imagine this is impossible to

40 ✳ Spirit of the Western Way

achieve. That is not the case. As you begin to express the desire to raise your vibration and change one thing in your diet with focus, love, and spiritual intention, your vibration will shift. As your vibration shifts, your desires will shift, for they are driven by your intentions and your thoughts and your focus. So make a concerted effort to change one basic element of your diet, such as meat, the most poisonous aspect of your intake. Start by halving your quantity and doubling your quality. This act alone will shift your vibration enough so that you will be amenable to shifting in other areas.

The Nonphysical Realm Can Help

This nutritional information is hard for you to understand because you think you are in charge of everything, and in some ways, that is true. It is a spiritual paradox. You are in charge of your focus, but when your focus becomes engaged with the spirit world to raise your vibration, we can help you from the nonphysical side. We do not intrude in any way; we merely respond to a desire for an increase in vibration. We can assist you in this area when you make the request. So this is the place to start: Make the request in your heart and mind, and focus on it.

When you go into a store to shop, pray for assistance from the non-physical. Ask us to assist you in choosing good foods. Listen to your guidance system — your feelings and your emotions — as you traverse the grocery store. Of course, we do not recommend doing this when you have small children in tow or are in a rush or are planning to prepare a meal for your boss or anything like that. Allow yourself an hour to quietly wander through the grocery store and to listen to your guidance system. We will speak to you through your guidance system. If you go into the shop with the idea of purchasing healthy food, this will transpire. You will be inspired by Spirit to offer more high-quality nutrition to your body.

Now, if you are starting from a North American diet that we mentioned previously, you have a long way to go. Understand that we in the nonphysical are not in a rush. Only you in the modern world are in a rush. If you take five years to change your diet and accomplish this goal, we will stand in applause on the sidelines of your spiritual evolution, cheering you on and happy for your progress. If you do not attempt this, five years down the line nothing will improve. You will be sicker, fatter, and in a worse place. But if you take tiny steps and our encouragement and allow yourself this gentle process of transformation, knowing that you have all the time in the world and that, as you raise your vibration, it will become easier and easier and easier, you will find this is a stress-free process. Only when you set arbitrarily high goals in the short term will you feel frustrated and become overwhelmed because you have not shifted your consciousness enough to shift your diet to that degree.

Identify Your Fears

As you shift your diet in small degrees, your beliefs will come up for healing and observation, and you will know that they have arisen because you will feel panic or conflict. When you panic and feel you need some particular food that you know is not the best for you, try to discern what the feeling is from. Is it fear of starvation? Is it fear of judgment? Is it some other deep-seated belief? Are you going to this food for love rather than nutrition? Throughout your childhood, you receive many emotions and hidden messages through food that come from your parents, your teachers, and the media.

You are very programmed creatures when it comes to food, and you must understand this as you go through the process of raising your food vibration. You cannot do it quickly; you are not free to choose what you wish. You think you are, but that is not the case. You have watched thousands of hours of food commercials. You have been punished by your parents at the dinner table, and you have been rewarded with food and love in combination, so you have confused many aspects of the energetic exchange with food. This is why it is such a difficult process to shift and such a difficult subject to understand, especially when you want to change and find that you repeatedly bump up against the same issues.

If something comes up repeatedly for you, it is probably linked to training your parents provided when you were a child. Perhaps they insisted that you give them a kiss when you wanted ice cream. These are the kinds of mind games that humans play with each other when it comes to food issues. You may have been tormented as a child for being fat or thin, and now you are terrified of being bullied if your body shape changes. Perhaps you think that if you lose control of your body, you will be attacked in some way. These are often deeply ingrained fears and beliefs held in the unconscious mind. As you shift your food emphasis, these beliefs will come up for observation. You do not need to force it. You do not need to be concerned that something that is out of sight and out of mind is undermining you. When there is something out of your conscious mind, it is not yet ready to be seen. You must trust the healing and transformation process. If you continue to approach it gently and with love, prayer, meditation, and connection to the nonphysical, you will be compassionately and surely guided to a diet that will elevate your vibration and connect you to higher realms that can assist you in many, many ways.

The ego has a direct relationship with food to preserve the body and survive, so it is a tricky area to change. The diet is deeply controlled by the ego mind because it is about physical survival. However, to attain the elevated vibrations of spiritual awareness that we seek for you so that you can come into your true nature and reach the potentials that you have contained within your mind, make this change with very high goals in mind.

Be gentle. This is not something that will be quick. The ego will be triggered if you push it too hard, and it will fight for its survival as any animal would. It is your animal programming, your physical programming, that is designed to keep the physical body alive. Remember what the body is. It is your representation of fear and separation, and when you begin to mess with its survival, it will attack. It is animalistic in this way and not spiritual in nature, so you must understand this association that the body triggers with the ego mind.

However, you can sanctify the body by raising the vibration of thought. We can help you raise the vibration of the body when you change what you eat and what you focus on. We can help you change the vibration of the body to assist in the shift of your consciousness. It is very difficult to shift your consciousness, and it is impossible to shift your consciousness more than a little bit if you are heavily immersed in eating bad foods that are polluted with pesticides. These are poisons, low in vibration, and heavy to the body. Our overall goal is to have you raise your consciousness so that you can achieve miraculous creativity, healing, and consciousness shifts. So food is a very important step.

You get the idea. Eat naturally occurring, unprocessed foods that are raw, if possible. We know that the cold climates some of you live in make this difficult, but that should be your ultimate goal. As we said, as you raise your vibration, your ability to choose will align with the higher vibration, and you will become more and more capable of things you currently cannot do. Just take it easy with yourself, and know what is at play here. The ego mind is very nervous when you start messing with its food, so change slowly and gently with love and awareness and with lots of prayer and meditation.

CHAPTER 6

Recondition Your Mind about Food

The positive aspects we ask you to participate in are very simple, but the incorrectly trained mind cannot make sound choices. Most of you have difficulty with food because your commercial and industrialized food production systems and the subsequent advertising systems convince you to eat those foods.

You are dealing with years and years of conditioning on what is healthy food and how to deal with the nutritional aspects of the physical world in which you live. You have been trained in an artificial system that tells you it is okay to eat food that is packaged in boxes and never rots. Maybe you were fed these as a child and were told they were good for you. Then you poured on a substance called milk (which we've already said is very cruelly raised and produced in your society and holds a frequency of fear and deprivation and murder), and you dig in to a bowl of cereal thinking, "Ah, this is good. My mother told me so."

You were indoctrinated very young and repeatedly. "Eat this up. It's good for you, dear one." You believed it — hook, line, and sinker — and you received love for doing it. You got a pat on the back as you trotted off to school after doing it. "Well done for eating up your breakfast!" You have gone through thousands of situations such as this with many of the foods you think of as healthy.

You are now confused that the mainstream media says dairy is not

46 ✳ Spirit of the Western Way

very good for you. Many of you are allergic or intolerant to it. Many of you who use alternative media are reading subversive and revolutionary material such as this. You hear that cereal and the milk you pour on it are not as good for you as you thought. From a psychological point of view, this causes stress because the new information falls on layers of conditioning about this food's healthy qualities. You must understand what has been done to you before you can truly change your mind, and you must change your mind before you can change your behavior.

So this is the difficulty that most of you face. You need to recondition your mind about food, and understand that it is going to take a little while to build the thought structures and beliefs about this new way of eating and what has been done to you in the past.

This has happened with many, many things. You have deep indoctrinations about meat and the body's need for it. You are blissfully ignorant of the conditions of the animals raised in your society, but we will not dwell on that. Instead, we will offer a solution. The solution we offer is scientifically proven: a plant-based, organic diet with more raw than cooked food is the best solution for your body's nutritional needs.

Pay Attention to Your Feelings

You will first question your conditioned beliefs and ideas about protein and the quantity of protein you need. Well, we can assure you that there is plenty of protein in nuts, seeds, grains, beans, and these kinds of foods. However, your conditioning about purchasing and preparing food will play into your problems with shifting to this new way of eating, so understand that you are deeply conditioned to eat what you eat. The way out of this problem is to evaluate your feelings when you begin to change something. We don't want you to change your diets across the board. This would cause too much stress because these deeply held belief structures drive your behavior and your eating habits.

When you start on this adventure to transform your diet, pick one thing to change at a time. As we mentioned earlier, if you eat a normal North American diet, we always recommend that you address the quantity and quality of meat that you eat. Why? It is the most poisonous and detrimental food you consume. It is very harsh on your environment because it uses enormous quantities of water and energy. The first thing

Recondition Your Mind about Food ✳ 47

to do is to halve the amount of meat you eat and double the quality by finding a supplier of local, organic, humanely raised meat, such as a local farm or a conscientious butcher and begin to support them. Yes, you will gasp when you see the price of the meat, but it is going to help your spiritual practice. You must deal with the emotions of that transaction. Deal with the feelings that come up in that moment.

Fear will come up because you will spend far more than your mind deems is okay. You will, perhaps, become fearful if you are in charge of meal preparation because you will have to deal with the wrath of the beings who are used to seeing a slab of meat on their plates at dinner or lunch or whatever. These feelings tell you about the structure of your mind, and this is where your spiritual practice is so very important to understand. It is not in the behavior alone where you will grow and heal; it is in dealing with these fears and emotions that arise as you counteract the conditioning your mind has been through. Most of these conditioning treatments are motivated by fear: fear of being a bad parent, fear of being a bad cook, fear of not providing proper nutrition, and so on.

As you begin to venture into diet transformation, understand that you will feel uncomfortable because you are breaking the rules of a society that deeply indoctrinated you to do as you are told, and you fear punishment. From what, you don't know. From whom, you don't know. All you know is that you feel fear.

These new ideas about food and transforming how you eat will cause anxiety because you have worn very deep trenches in the physical brain structure. The old ways of thinking literally created ruts that you are overwhelmingly motivated to continue to follow, and the new ideas, thoughts, and understandings must create new pathways in the brain. That will also be a little uncomfortable. Understand that these basic principles will be at play. Choose one thing at a time to deal with so that you can process the feelings and get to the beliefs beneath those negative emotions, and then you can change the beliefs.

When you go shopping after reading this chapter, find an ethical butcher or a local farmer (if you are fortunate enough to have access to that), and process the emotions related to that subject. After you shop there, once you begin putting in your orders for your wholesomely raised

48 ✳ Spirit of the Western Way

meat products, remember to cut down the frequency you eat them by 50 percent initially. Then you can choose to change something else.

After that, we recommend changing the amount of dairy products you put into your body because dairy products, as meat products, have been heavily marketed as necessary in your diet. They are not necessary in your diet. The bone-building chemicals you need and the vitamins that are promoted in milk can be found in naturally occurring nuts, seeds, grains, vegetables, and these kinds of things. Once again, milk marketing has been used to control populations and to indoctrinate mothers, in particular, into force-feeding milk to their children.

These huge shifts in your consciousness are required for your ascension, so look at it that way. We repeat: It is not just about the food; it is about the beliefs that these foods support. This is literally how you will gain your freedom. If you do not change the beliefs you hold and if you continue to battle the behavior you are trying to assert with thoughts such as, "This food is not nutritious enough. I am not going to get enough protein," or "My bones are going to get weak because I'm not drinking milk," when you buy healthy food, you will not be able to maintain that behavior. The behavior you experience each day rises from your belief system, and if your belief system is counter to your behavior, you will feel very stressed and confused, and you will not be able to maintain the behavior we ask you to maintain. So deal with the feelings and the thoughts as part of this transformative practice as you change your diet.

Know Making Changes Will Become Easier

Now, changing your diet will take some time, and you will find certain things are so deeply conditioned in you that you seem completely powerless to change them. As you go through this process, little by little, you will change the belief structure you have about food. Your body will become healthier, your frequency will go up, and you will be able to make choices you currently cannot make. Do not judge yourself in this moment for not being able to go immediately to a completely healthy diet as we describe it.

A completely healthy diet is the kind of diet that you would have had 200 years ago, such as foods raised on small farms without chemicals and with love in a community-based fashion. Examples include organic meats as well as organic eggs from chickens allowed to run in the yard in the sun as they eat worms and scratch. They are happy creatures who, even when they are harvested, are loved and respected as providers of wonderful, wonderful nutrition.

That is a dream as far as most of you are concerned, but as you support these farmers and organic food growers, you demonstrate your understanding of the poisonous nature of your current industrialized food production systems. Put your money where you want more growth. Support those beings who are on the leading edge of saving your health. Help those beings who have the courage and the spiritual inspiration to grow organic and naturally healthy foods for you to eat, and do not support the big companies who mass-produce poisonous foods. You must, as you step into a supermarket or store, understand that you are the source of money and energy that these large companies rely on, and if you refuse to support them, if you refuse to hand over your hard-earned money, then you will make a bold and loving statement not only to your family, your body, and your health but also to this beautiful planet you live on.

As you deal with these issues and food products, you will find the inspiration further helps you to transform your diet. Do not allow yourself to be attacked by the ego mind, which will say that you must do it all now, that you must conform or become perfect. It will tell you to either not do it or do it all at once. We propose a slow and steady psychological transformation that helps support healthy choices and behaviors, and this takes time because a lot of time, money, and effort have been put into conditioning your mind. We must remind you of that as you step into these new behaviors and thought patterns.

So take it easy, dear ones. First change your meat and then your dairy intake. That is a lot for most of you because you have strong addictions to those foods, and you will have your work cut out for you. We will deal with these subjects throughout the next few years, so you will have lots more information, but the truth is this: Imagine a farm 200 years ago, and choose what you eat based on what you would find there, which is very simple. There were very few cardboard boxes, no aluminum trays, and no freezers. The food was naturally grown, organic, locally produced, and perhaps even traded.

CHAPTER 7

Release Addictions to Find Freedom

Your society is very fond of caffeinated drinks. Our dear channel has a challenge in this area. Coming from an English background, she is very fond of tea, a source of great comfort in that culture. Tea was given when she was sad, happy, or needed comfort and love. It was given at every opportunity, so it has a deeply ingrained association with positive emotions for her.

In North America, the caffeinated beverage with emotional associations is typically coffee. It is associated with waking up, getting to work, and being productive — quick, on the ball, or at the top of your game. Of course, these unconscious beliefs are associated with success and financial reward. However, caffeine is addictive, and perhaps you add sugar, which also creates dependency. What you do not realize is that you are not really free.

It is easy to consider these substances as mere simple pleasures, but the truth is they are a driving force in your behavior, and until you are truly free of them, you will not be free to make your own choices. Most of you are not aware of this loss of freedom. You think you choose to go to the coffee shop each morning and enjoy that first sip as the nectar of life itself, but you are addicted. This is the reality. Many of you will roll your eyes and say, "I am not giving up my coffee. I am not giving up my tea. It is beyond ridiculous to even entertain this idea!" We are speaking about the

52 ✳ Spirit of the Western Way

ideal here. Do you wish to stop suffering? Do you wish to attain incredible health? Do you wish to achieve creative expression that is beyond your wildest dreams? This is not about your coffee or your tea; this is about issues that are far greater and far more exciting than these habits that really do not add to your life.

In some ways, these things give you small pleasures that make your life tolerable. If you actually let them go, you would realize that greater changes need to be made, but as long as you get these little pick-me-ups throughout the day, you think your life is perhaps worth living and that you can keep going. If you were to take caffeine out of your diet, it's true that you would feel the loss. You would feel discomfort, but you would understand that you were seeking tiny pleasures throughout the day to keep you going in a life that many of you do not really enjoy very much. If you were to remove these things, you would see your discontent, and you would begin to shift. You would make some tangible changes in your life that would bring you far more satisfaction than a sip of coffee.

Of course, this also applies in a more magnified way to alcohol consumption. Alcohol is used systematically in your culture to numb the desire for change. It is used to numb boredom and to access joy when you do not know how to access it naturally.

Don't Medicate Your Guidance System

For many of you, the workaday world is stressful. You have long commutes and busy lives and homes, and your drink at the end of the day or that bottle of wine on a Friday night is such a welcome release from your life that to even think of stopping is blasphemous in your mind. But these addictive drinks — your coffees, teas, and alcoholic beverages — are medications you use to keep your vibration low and to provide little doses of relief in a world that is actually very dissatisfying to you.

These issues that require your attention, these dissatisfactions, are medicated by these small inputs of information on a regular basis. The bigger issues are terrifying for you to entertain, and we understand that. We are not trying to gloss over the difficulties of your lives, but understand that you are self-medicating. It is as if you are taking small doses of anesthesia all the time so that you do not feel pain. However, your emotional guidance system that tells you how you feel all the time is a blessing. It is your spirit trying to speak to you, the map of your destiny conversing with you. If you continue to numb it, it is as if you are repeatedly throwing a blanket over a fire: It creates a lot of smoke and mess, and you won't be warmed. You cannot experience the comfort of the fire.

The passions, desires, hopes, and dreams that you have in your heart — this true self that wishes to express itself through action, creativity, communion, and communication — always speaks to you. The addiction to caffeine and alcohol is an epidemic in your culture because sadness and disillusionment are epidemics in your culture. You cannot continually function in a disillusioned, disappointed, sad, depressed way without medicating yourself. It is impossible.

Your body is designed to lead you out of trouble and to show you the path to bliss, and that is what your guidance system tells you. If you need a double martini on a Friday night to get out of your mind — to recover from your work, your marriage, your home, or whatever it is that's causing the burden — you are medicating your guidance system. Your guidance system tells you where things are wrong, and often it tells you how to fix the problem. However, the longer you medicate, the worse the problem gets, the deeper the sadness becomes, and the more health issues you face.

The Body Adjusts to Your Appetites

Your culture tells you that addictions are related to the substances you ingest. Now, this is true in some ways. It is the body's nature to acclimatize to what you give it, and this is one of its most wonderful adaptive qualities. If you live on fish and chips, it will say, "Okay, we will live on fish and chips and do the best we can with that." If you are carnivorous and eat lots of meat, it will do its best to survive and thrive in that environment, but it will be difficult. However, what you do not realize is that addiction is driven by the mind.

Remember, the mind has created the body to house its fears, to represent its idea of separation, and to project so that the mind is allowed some peace. The body was created so that the mind can find some peace from its fears and perceived guilt. It projects guilt onto others to feel better, and it attacks the body and uses addiction as a way to store negative energy. This is a very adaptive behavior. The mind cannot live with all its problems, issues, fears, terrors, and resentments, so it tries to put them in safe places to have some kind of normal functionality. It is not a maladaptive process. However, if you wish to reach the higher realms of spiritual development, you must walk up to these frightening little Pandora's boxes, lift the lids, and see what is inside. Then you must take out the contents and love what you find.

We do not attack anything here. All solutions come to fruition through love, acceptance, and forgiveness. That is the practice. Forgiveness represents your understanding that you project your thoughts into your world and into your body, and those projections are aspects of you that you must bring back to the fold. You must reintegrate them in your mind through loving kindness, forgiveness, and compassion for yourself and others. This is why these practices are so important within our teaching, for the physical act represents your comprehension of these principles.

When a person is addicted, something that is very painful and disruptive for the mind is projected into the body and offered up as a sacrifice, if you will, to this fear. The person will medicate this concept of hatred (often for the self or another) and unforgiveness with a substance.

Some substances that you use to cover these fears and guilt and projections of the mind include food, alcohol, shopping, gossip, work, and exercise, to name some. We can go on and on about how you medicate yourselves. Many of you do not see it. You see the heroin addict on the street as different from you. However, many of you are not at peace in your minds. Peace is not something you really understand because of the structure of your society and what it emphasizes as valuable. You are trained to not listen to your guidance systems. You are trained to avoid quiet and contemplative activities, and you are trained to shun spiritual practice, ways many humans used to resolve their problems.

Spiritual seekers used to understand that a loss of peace was an internal condition caused by a spiritual problem. Of course, this is the case because everything you do is spiritual. You are all on spiritual paths; you just do not know it. You are repeatedly told that you are bodies and that your bodies are valuable but fallible. You are repeatedly told that there is no god, no purpose. Even when you are involved in spiritual activities, many of you continue to project your ideas of spirituality onto the physical world, and you make the physical world sacred. You must remember you created the physical world to house your negativities. In that sense, it is not sacred, but you can turn the nightmare into a happy dream.

The true purpose of spiritual growth and of your birth is to wake up. That is the reason you are here. It is not to accumulate millions of dollars, to perfect your body, or to convert others to any particular religion or activity. Your purpose in being born is to remove the blocks in your mind to love's presence so that you can become peaceful, and in your peace, you can connect to knowledge, receive information and guidance, and wake up.

Addictions are detrimental to this process, for they allow you to blame something for your lack of peace when it is actually your own mind that is not at peace. Addictions must be dealt with through spiritual practices. That is the only way to effect change of a significant nature in the mind so that you can relinquish the physical substance you use for relief from the disturbances that constantly run through your thoughts.

Addictions Arise to Lead to Awareness

You recognize behaviors that are not nutritious and are detrimental to your life. They might be gambling, having sex, or watching television. The latter is a terrible addiction in your society, and it is how most beings medicate their minds. They lie in front of this device of hypnosis and allow it to take over their brain waves. Embedded within this addiction are messages of fear from your governing bodies, messages to overconsume food and obsess on the physical body. These messages come to you fast and furiously through this addiction, and they cause increased dissatisfaction and self-loathing while encouraging other addictions, such as shopping, eating, or exercising.

If you are addicted to something, focus on why. Are there particular circumstances that cause the behavior? For many of you, the cause fades, deeply pushed into the unconscious mind, and you simply repeat a behavior associated with certain times, people, or places. Recognizing these connections is the best way to begin breaking an addiction and to subtly shift where and how you do it. For example, if you always have a cigarette at a certain time, postpone that cigarette for five minutes, and feel the body's and the mind's craving for that substance.

Many of you do not really realize how addicted you are until you start to shift the time that you ingest the substance and actually experience how terribly, terribly agitated you become. You tell yourself, "I don't have a drinking problem. I drink. I get drunk. I fall down. No problem!" This is essentially what many of you do with your addictions, and you do not realize that you are driven by them. Do not approach them too quickly. You use them to achieve some relief from the mind, so you must approach them with some reverence.

To go cold turkey can cause agitation and a reaction that is difficult to handle. The reaction will arise regardless of how quickly or slowly you remove the habit from your daily activities. We suggest a gentler and more concerted effort to be aware of the activity rather than just ending it unless, of course, you are involved in a dangerous addiction such as to sex, drugs, or alcohol. These are very detrimental and life threatening, and they require professional assistance. There are systems in your society that assist beings in this way.

If you are addicted, you cannot continue into the higher peaceful, miraculous, and angelic spiritual realms until these issues are dealt with in a meaningful way. Remember, you seek relief from pain within the mind, and through this knowledge, you can forgive yourself and understand that the behavior arose from actually caring about your mind, your sanity, and your ability to function.

Recognize where you are out of control. The issue will be reflected in some aspect of your life, such as your marriage, weight, criminal behavior, and so on. You will see where the problem is, and you will realize that there is a pattern you created. The world and all the issues you have in it are yours. They represent aspects of your mind that you are not aware of, and they rise up so that you can heal it with awareness, love, forgiveness, and compassion. This awareness will allow you to approach the addiction in a much more forgiving and loving way. Through loving and forgiving activities, all things are healed. Things do not heal when you attack them. Relationships are not healed through yelling. Only through love, forgiveness, and understanding can the mechanisms of the mind be healed. Everything is mind. Everything is mind. Everything is mind. Do not think about it in any other way. Your entire life is your mind manifesting for you to see.

CHAPTER 8

Reconsider Your Mind's Nutrition

Nutrition is what you put into your body, believing that it feeds you in some way. Let's approach the subject of education as a form of nutrition. The education systems in Western society have been both detrimental to your spiritual growth and beneficial to your intellectual growth. We understand that some of you have had privileged childhoods and others have had very poor, underprivileged childhoods. The vast majority of you went to primary schools, middle schools, high schools, and perhaps even universities. We speak of the general Western education.

Children come into this system very early in life — too early, as far as we can see, for the best spiritual development. Children at four and five and six years old are still in a very active and magical stage of dreaming. We call it dreaming; it is not actually living in that sense. They are in a dream world of their own where fantasies and friendships and memories of the nonphysical are still at play. They can entertain themselves with games, endlessly frolicking, running, and jumping. To go to school at the early age of five years old, on average, is quite detrimental. A little being who is very free flowing in consciousness is forced into a rigid structure when, in fact, that free-flowing consciousness would continue much longer if it were allowed. Children are put in this situation, and their guidance systems are affected. They have to go where they do not wish to go. They have to get up in the morning and wear clothes that perhaps they do not wish to wear, and the rigid structure is placed on their magical minds and begins to thwart their desires. They learn that there are things they must do that they do not wish to do, and of course, this is the basic problem in your society. Very early on, your desire for freedom and creativity is thwarted, and the mind is trained with information and details that promote obsession with the past and the future.

These are all things that bring suffering later on. Of course, nobody does this on purpose. Nobody educates a child as a means of punishment. You send your children to school because you think it is good for them. Parents are taught that to do so is right. The laws reinforce that it is right, so you all participate in the conditioning program. There is an obsession with the past, an obsession with control, and an obsession with conformity. There are, of course, those beings who slip through the cracks because their talents and skills do not match conformity, regulation, or linear thinking. The best creatives in the world and brilliant mathematical minds do not do well in school because they are out of alignment with the mediocrity that is promoted. Remember, your school systems were designed to produce workers, people who will do as they are told and produce work while an authority figure tells them what to do.

From a creative and spiritual point of view, this is far from the best situation. Over time, little spirits are knocked into shape, formed into those nice squares, and they become deeply entrenched in the belief that if they do not receive certain grades, they are not worthy. Parents support this. They ask their children about their school day when they return home, and if the child is not high up on the roster, then a disappointed look crosses the parent's face. The child begins to see that lovability is directly related to success in school. This training is very powerful (you know this), and as the young progress further and further into the school system, the rigidity and the focus narrow further, and all the qualities of humanity become less and less important as they are groomed for the work force.

The Past Isn't the Way to a Better Future

You could consider this education a form of nutrition, but it is a very bland diet for the mind, the heart, the body, and the spirit. You typically have thirteen years of conditioning, and many of you have another four or eight years added to that, further narrowing your focus from the nonphysical to the physical, the past, the material, and the historical. And remember that many of the things you are taught simply are not true! They provide one point of view that may be taken if you so choose, but there are no teachings of anything metaphysical or emotional that are related to consciousness. You are systematically drawn away from that which is the most nutritious part of your world and life, and you suffer. The stress of the high school student who faces exams is a good example, and the peer pressure to conform is very difficult for young minds. You hear that young beings who do not fit in at school sometimes commit suicide, and you can see that this is a very distressing route that your society forces beings to take.

The upside of this system is that you are given a lot of information, you become literate, and you can communicate with each other. These are wonderful things — learning to write, to read, and to educate yourself — so we are not being negative here; we simply want you to understand what you face when you come into the arena of reeducation that we ask you to enter. You must understand what has happened to you so that you can be aware of your limitations in thinking and why you feel discomfort as we push you into areas your culture has told you not to explore. Understand this conditioning process so that when you feel uncomfortable about where we ask you to go, you understand why. If you do not understand why, you will mistakenly interpret that your guidance system is telling you not to go there and for good reason. In fact, you think you are told not to go there because you have been taught not to go there. It is merely a discomfort rather than a directive from your guidance system.

This guidance system is a gift from God and the map out of the mire of delusion in which you have voluntarily put yourself. You have voluntarily put yourself in this world through a desire to experience individuality and separation. Of course, school represents a wonderful form of individuality and separation in that sense. You can sit at your desk by yourself in your own world and be separate from everybody. You can, indeed, feel inferior and alone. School can be a powerful reinforcing factor of these belief structures that you come to this world with.

Many authority figures who you have been taught to listen to and believe have, in fact, fed you erroneous information. They have taught you that history is important, whereas we say it's important to not revisit history. Stay in the present, and keep your mind on its creative trajectory based on the present moment into the immediate future, allowing thoughts and ideas to flow through your mind and to offer you stimulation to create new ideas and new experiences. If you are obsessed with historical dates and events of the past, you are drawn deeper into the illusion, which wants you to believe in linear time. The past is very important in creating, and the ego mind is entrenched in this falsity that your past creates your future. You think that if you keep looking at your past, you will become safer and you will learn how you got into the pickle you are in. This is, of course, the opposite of what we tell you.

The higher mind will tell you to forget about the past because it was created by the level of consciousness you were at then. If you wish to create a different expression in your future, you must raise your vibration in the present and focus on something of a higher level. Only then will your future be different. So the part of your education process that always refers to history undermines your ability to create a new future. School also teaches you that the world is objective, and you have nothing to do with it. We teach you the opposite.

Embrace Your Special Gifts

Retain the best of your education, which is the ability to read and write (these are magnificent tools in the reeducation process) and some of the other disciplines you learned in school, such as the ability to sit for a few hours at a desk to do some particular work or to create some particular painting. The insistence on learning facts is not as important. It is much more important to be immersed in your imagination.

The education you have received about conformity is incorrect. You are all very different and very special in the gifts that you have been given. To stand out or to not fit in is, in fact, a great boon and a great reflection on your alignment with your true nature, which is absolutely unique. No one is more special in God's eyes than anyone else, but your individual skills, talents, strengths, and passions are your own. They are a complete and absolutely unique pattern that is yours, and it is yours for a reason: You are designed to have a particular purpose, and your qualities suit that purpose very well.

For example, if you focus intently and enjoy studying, you might find that you are destined to be a research scientist who assists in some great discovery. If you are musical and freethinking, music might be your passion, and conformity will not support your life's purpose. You might have great difficulty joining in groups and conforming to structures. Your culture might deem these as negative, as poor qualities, but in your destiny as a musician, you might find that they allow you to focus on creating music in your own style and in your own way.

Pay attention to your natural traits. Have you been trained to sit still all the time and be inactive when you think you'd like to run? Does it go against what you have been taught, so you do not do it? Perhaps the idea of running continually comes up, and you think, "It would feel wonderful to run," but you never do. Pay attention to these ideas that well up from underneath all the conditioning, and understand the education and conditioning that you have been through so that you can discern the difference between your true nature and your conditioned mind. You will have to unravel this a little bit. If you have been in a deeply repressive religious school, for example, understand that all those teachings you receive from a very young age are regimented and repeatedly reinforced, so you have a lot of conditioning to confront.

This conditioning manifests in your mind as conflict because you have a natural state of being that arises from your true nature, from your spiritual essence. This is your creative self — your self-expression — that wishes to come out, but the teachings from your school system conflict with that. You might want to be freer and more creative than you are allowing yourself to be. Perhaps you have become a policing force. The conditioned mind could be layered over your true desires so that you are in conflict with yourself. The voice may sound like your mother or the teacher or the religious instruction you have had, but you have become the enforcer of rules, and it causes conflict within the mind. You will feel the conflict as a lasting desire that is constantly thwarted by some other aspect of yourself, so it is not hard to find. Such conflicts in the mind will center on your desires for creativity, self-expression, physical activity, and so on.

Set aside some time to write down the name of the schools you went to and the memories you have of them. This is a brief excursion into your

62 ✳ Spirit of the Western Way

history, and we will not stay there long, but it is important that you consciously recall these memories and think about them. What was your most traumatic experience with a teacher there? What did you enjoy about school? What was your favorite subject, and what was your most difficult subject? Did you have social interactions that were pleasing, or were you traumatized by peer pressure and groups of friends or enemies you encountered on this journey?

This is very important for you to revisit. It is part of the nutrition you were fed through your education system. We call it nutrition because it is part of the material from which you are built, and it is very important. When you eat a very bad diet, your body reflects that. You then realize you need to be compassionate with yourself and give yourself time to shift for a different result. You have had the same experience in your education system. You have been fed a certain kind of educational "food," and your body-mind complex is a result of that. When that is out of alignment with your true nature and desires, you have to reeducate yourself and put sound nutrition in your body-mind complex. This will help you get back to a state of equilibrium and a positive association with who you really are.

We speak of who you are in a physical human sense, but there is a higher "who you are" that really has nothing to do with this physical manifestation you are experiencing. We are working on layers. We wish to help you remove the most painful layers of your conditioning so that you can experience your life in a more positive way rather than live through the conditioned mind, which is very, very limiting and painful at times because of this conflict with your deeper nature that wishes to express itself. You are here to experience that self and come to an understanding of who you are.

Many of you live lives that are not authentic in even the most basic sense. You live the conditioned teachings of a society that wishes to limit you, control you, judge you, and keep you in a very small area of acceptability. Take ten minutes to do the following exercise.

As you write about your school experience, take the information about your traumas, your joys, your strengths, your weaknesses, and the things you had difficulty with into your conscious mind. Mull that over a little bit to see whether you can determine where these things manifest in your life. If you were denigrated in the classroom as a young child, do you believe and still tell yourself that you are not acceptable in some way?

This results of this exercise will vary for each of you. It is a personal exercise, something that you must do to come to an understanding of yourself, and it is important. A very deeply ingrained aspect of the mind has been shifted by your culture, and when you realize that, you can change it and come to some understanding of what has happened. You can recognize what you do not like about what has happened, and you can shift your focus and your internal dialogue.

The conditioned mind manifests as an internal dialogue that carries the voice of authority and judgment and limitation. It will not make you feel good, and it will be out of alignment with the loving voice of All That Is that urges you on to greatness, to self-love and communion with your fellow travelers on this spiritual journey. The conditioned mind's voice is negative, and perhaps our little exercise you will help you to discern what kind of education nutrition you have had. If it's been a bad diet, what can you do to shift that nutrition?

Educate Yourself about Your Passion

Take the wonderful skills of reading and writing that you learned in school, and employ them on your journey to awakening. What nutrition will you put into your mind, knowing that you have been conditioned and have had these negative experiences and teachings that focus on the material world and offer a limited view and restrictive consequences?

Read material that is aligned with the inner self, the person within you who you would like to bring out, the person whose dreams you would like to reanimate, the discouraged person you would like to encourage, the person you would like to nurture who was attacked. What does this being inside you — this dear, sweet being who was born unto this world to live freely and self-expressively — want to learn? Does it want to learn how to ride a horse? Does it want to learn how to paint? Does it want to learn how to become a musician or to speak a different language? There are many ideas in your mind that will repeatedly surface if you have not completely killed off your inner self through conditioning. Some people

64 ✳ Spirit of the Western Way

have indeed done that, but they are probably not reading this book if they are in the dire straits of deep unconsciousness.

Borrow books from the library, or educate yourself through the Internet, which has wonderful material at your fingertips twenty-four hours a day. Do this instead of using it for mindless entertainment and gossip gathering. Listen to your inner voice that is asking you to do something. You all have it. Look up from your forty-hour workweek or from the life that you say is not really what you want, and listen to the voice in you that whispers for you to grow flowers or take a great trek across the Asian continent or to have some other wonderful adventure. Read and write about these subjects that excite you.

Do you have a dream in your heart? Do you think, "Ah, if I were to win the lottery, 'this' is what I would do. If I had free will, I would become 'this'"? You can become what you would like to be. You can shift your consciousness to such a degree that your world reflects your desire. Now, many of you will say, "This is impossible! I have a mortgage. I have a family. I have all of these restrictions and limitations that I have chosen." We remind you that you chose them. Part of your mind, the conditioned part, chose them. If you feel imprisoned by those choices now, then you chose things that are not your heart's desire. Understand that it is your responsibility to yourself and to your spiritual evolution to follow your heart's desire.

If you have caused people to rely on you, we do not suggest you abandon them. However, do not continue to abandon yourself, and use this education process in which you have been trained to do certain positive things to build a passionate focus and life. Given the life you've been living, you might at first sneak these new things in as dirty little secrets because they are far removed from what you are living and the people you are around. This too reflects on your separation from your true nature. If your desire is out of accord with what people believe you are, then you are out of accord with what you are. You will not be happy or healthy. You will not thrive when you do not listen to an aspect of yourself that is passionately interested in something. This is a very important turning point in this subject. Use your education skills to focus on something you wish to learn.

We want you to develop a hobby and a library of some kind. You could purchase books on this particular subject if you feel that this is what you wish to do. You might bookmark particular articles and videos and lessons on your computer, but we would actually like you to have some tangible representations of your dreams in your life. Perhaps gather images of things you are interested in. Let's say you are interested in gardens. You can collect paintings or photographs of spectacular gardens and even purchase a coffee-table book about them. When you bring your passion to life within your own experience, you will find that focusing on something you love will create energy around it, and you will begin to manifest experiences that give you the opportunity to magnify this.

This is how creation works. This is how your life is made. If you are living a life you do not enjoy, you have repeatedly focused your mind in a direction that has made that world. Do not berate or punish yourself, and do not judge anyone else for causing this. You have done it through your focus. It might have been involuntary; you might have been forced into it by outside energies. The fact is you can change it because you are the creator of your world. We insist you understand this. You are the creator of your world, and you get out of your life what you put into it. So you can, at this very moment as you read this sentence, begin to shift your consciousness in a direction that will bring you more satisfaction, more happiness, and more health and vitality.

We end this chapter with that prescription: Take a moment. What is it that you dream of doing? Where does your mind drift to when you give it absolute freedom? What is your passion? Some of you may be more in touch with that than others; some of you know exactly what you would like to do. Increase that passion. Keep going toward it if it draws you. Keep going to it, enjoy it, make no excuses for it, and make more time for it in your day. Get up earlier if you have to. Take a little longer lunch or the long way home from work if you have to. Pay more attention to it, and if you feel you need to, explain your actions to your partner in crime, your lover, your cocreator on this journey. Explain what you are doing so that he or she does not feel attacked. This is not an attack on your life; it is merely your effort to get back in touch with a part of yourself that has become separate and that you would like to re-embrace with your heart and your time and your focus.

CHAPTER 9

Books, Television, and Films as Nutrition for the Mind

On this journey of reconditioning the mind, be careful about what you read, for the mind has a tendency to believe as fact whatever is put into it. For example, it will read a murder novel as if it is real. The information is accepted as verified even though you might, in your conscious mind, know it is a story about a fictitious murder. The details and descriptive natures of these books give the mind (the ego mind in particular) ideas and thoughts that will recur. An author might describe a dark and stormy night and a character who is at home listening to the floors creak and doors rattle. If the passage is written with great ability and passion, those images appear in the mind, and it will recall them on a dark and stormy night when you are in your house, and you will become frightened. You might not necessarily associate it with the novel you read several weeks before, but information goes into the mind all the time. Think about what you put in there. Make an effort at this point in your development to find out what the barriers are to your spiritual development so that you can achieve a higher level of accomplishment in creativity and spiritual openness. It is important that you put in truthful information that will assist you.

The wisdom texts of the ancients, translations of spiritual material, are good things to read. However, the Bible is full of violence and untruth, and we prefer that it is not the book you read. This is going to upset some

68 ✳ Spirit of the Western Way

of you, of course, but there is much untruth in that book. If you are interested in reading Christian doctrine and the teachings of the one you call Jesus, study *A Course in Miracles* and read the texts produced by us and our dear channel. These are Jesus's teachings, unadulterated by archaic traditions and the agendas of religious and political leaders who manipulate documents to fulfill their own desires. There is much information there that can shift consciousness and show the way out of darkness.

It is a difficult read, and not every mind can align with it, but there are many modern spiritual books that talk about the mind. *A Course in Miracles* is a nondualistic text that speaks about truth in all its forms. (Many other books do not speak about the world in the way that it is truly formed.) From there, you will find other things that align with the teachings. This is the best way to go about reeducating the mind: to study, for some time, something based on truth. Very few texts on your planet are based on truth.

You live in a dualistic world that appears to be of light and dark, good and evil, and life and death, yet this is not your true experience. *A Course in Miracles* provides a shift in consciousness because you actually begin to see the world in a way that is aligned with truth, and then you begin to understand other things. There are many derivatives of it, but they tend to be based in the dualistic view of the world that it is true reality and that you are indeed a body. You are not a body, and this is not your true reality. It is a manufactured representation of your psychology, and consequently, if your psychology is out of alignment with truth, you will not see the truth represented. You will see untruths, and your thought processes will be confused and divergent in nature. We are trying to align you with truth so that you can create truth in your life, your body, your day, and your consciousness. So you can see this is a tricky subject. We do not wish to restrict you only to our books and *A Course in Miracles*, but if you wish to comprehend the truth, these are good places to start. After you digest those materials, you will have better discernment and be able to choose other things that are more palatable in terms of our and your requirements. If you wish to wake up, this is what you must understand: As long as you feed yourself untruth, you will not develop in the way you wish to develop, into a being that is at peace and, in that state of peace, aligned with knowledge and able to communicate with the nonphysical in an easy and open way.

Television Feeds the Consumer Mentality

Western television- and movie-watching habits are a challenge for Spirit. Television is the worst element of your society that we have to deal with at this time. It has become a disseminator of hypnotic, trance-inducing material. Many of you have one in each room of your house, and when you leave those rooms, you take another device with you on which you can continue to watch information to keep the hypnotic trance going when you are on a bus, in a waiting room, and even at work.

When you watch television, you enter into deep, slow brain waves. This passive way of watching is designed to keep you enthralled, to relax you, and open your mind, which is the most dangerous aspect about it. The images, sounds, colors, and dialogues that take place on the screen are designed to entice you, and once you are in a world of make-believe, the lower mind is where you function in a subconscious way. All the information you watch goes in. You are not alert. All you have to do is look at the eyes of someone who is enthralled with a program to know that he or she is not very present. Of course, this is why you are so deeply hooked on consumer society and belief in the body, beauty, and values of your system. You cannot imagine not receiving this information on a daily basis.

Some people (and many of you reading this book could be among that group) recognize the detrimental effect that television has on the vibrational system and realize that those who watch television eat too much and become fearful because they make associations. But there are millions upon millions upon millions of beings who have no idea what is going on, and they are sad, overweight, and depressed. They do not realize that the thing they go to every night to bring them relief from their stress is what is creating that stress. They are inexorably and repeatedly taught to buy things, worry about what they are driving, worry about what shape their bodies are in, and so on, and they relentlessly empty the coffers of their lives in an effort to attract love.

That is the message you are taught: If you look a certain way and own certain things, you will have love. The need for love is the most primal drive because you are beings of love and you know you are out of alignment with love. Therefore, in your culture, you fall for the tale that if you do only "this," "that," or "the other," love will come your way. You

70 ＊ Spirit of the Western Way

are love, and you are able to connect with love, but you must remove all these objects and beliefs to align with love. This is the saddest part for us to see. You all do these things, spending all this money and believing it will bring you love, when in fact, these misperceptions keep the message and the experience of love out of your lives. Television is a very dangerous recreational activity.

Seek Entertainment in Other Places

When surfing the Internet, you can choose to watch a variety of inspired material (although commercials are infiltrating that too, which is a shame, but you have the option to ignore them). While searching the Internet, you can find documentaries about subjects you are interested in, listen to inspired lectures from great teachers, and learn about alternative ideas pertaining to reality. This is wonderful. We suggest you go there for your entertainment while you reeducate yourself. If you have a television in your house, especially if you have children, begin the process of weaning. We would like you to begin the process of shifting emphasis from this draining and hypnotic activity to more educational, life-giving, and life-affirming activities.

Many of the shows on television are about the body: decorating it, appreciating it, lusting after it, and destroying it. The ego trip has no bounds on this thing you watch every night. Your news is worst of all. You think you are educating yourself when you watch it. In fact, you are being indoctrinated into a cult of attack and war and death when you believe the story that is told that there is no other way, no option in your world, than to blow each other up. We come at this time with these teachings because you are, indeed, about to blow yourselves to kingdom come! There is another way to get to kingdom come, and that is through the mind, through mental and emotional comprehension, discipline, and study.

Do not turn your television on without thinking about it. Do not enter into that hypnotic trance. When we see people watching television, it is as if corpses are lying on the couch; that is the level of spiritual awakening in that activity. You are better served by taking a bath and hopping into bed with a good book. We can communicate with you there, and we can assist you in your waking. We do not suggest that you stop cold turkey. The mind that has been hypnotized in this way will not be peaceful; it will be agitated when it cannot get the information it is used to receiving.

A deep addiction forms through serialized shows, so do not watch new series. They are designed to tap you into the next one and the next one and the next one, and nothing really happens in them. You are much better served by sitting down to watch a movie that has a good story and beautiful production and sound. This is a much better thing to do. Better yet, develop habits of exercise, contemplation, and education.

This is a big arena for you. It is hard for you to imagine living without your habits, and this one is your biggest. Look around your home. If a large television is front and center, you can truly comprehend that you are separate from love, peace, self-awareness, and conscious contact with the nonphysical because of that device. That device is the major cause of depression, fear, and self-loathing in your society. Do not look at it as your friend. It is not your friend: it is an enemy, and it will not bring you what you wish.

Violent Films Fuel the Ego Mind

Movies are another great cultural institution in the Western world that puts much information in the mind. The violent, hero-driven blockbuster movie is fodder for the Western mind; other genres also affect your peace of mind and ability to be happy.

In blockbuster movies, an alien force is invariably about to invade, and the hero, through a series of serendipitous events, is "forced" to use violence. This is the theme, and it does not vary that much. In fact, we are sometimes quite amused by how you watch the same story over and over again with different characters or even puppets playing the roles, and you seem to be endlessly entertained. Of course, *you* are not endlessly entertained; the ego is endlessly entertained.

As your culture taps into the ego mind through these subjects, it becomes fascinated with bloodletting and self-righteously annihilating the bad guy. You must remember, this is what your world is designed to do. It is designed to separate you from the other, from the bad things within your mind that frighten you, such as ideas of judgment and hatred. It is designed to project all this hatefulness onto others, creating the good guy–bad guy scenario. So as you innocently go into a movie

72 ✳ Spirit of the Western Way

theater and buy your popcorn — supplying yourself with foods you do not need [smiles] to keep you amused in a theater that is providing you with entertainment that you do not need (we are joking with you here, of course) — you are unaware of the suffering that this entertainment causes. It reinforces the separation myth and brings that idea through in full color and surround sound and with very great special effects. Of course, when people come out of a theater experience such as that, they have no idea what they have done to themselves. They have immersed themselves in the ego mind using powerful images and sound associations, and this disrupts their lives! If people knew what they were doing, they would not go to these movies and feed the ego mind that is so destructive.

Every person who sees a violent movie in which bodies are destroyed has his or her mind warped by that information. The viewer takes it in, and it feeds the thought structures within the ego mind. The ego mind contains thought structures of violence (such as decapitation, disembowelment, and so on), and they have their own energy. When millions and millions of beings are immersed in these images and have them implanted in their consciousnesses, their ego minds are fed. It is like feeding a monster, and it indeed gains power.

When you look around your world at your reactions to disruptions, what do you see? You are faced with it in Syria, with the violence that has been perpetrated on the beings in that country. You insist on treating the world with violence. This is no accident. This is how the movies end and how the heroes win. It is an idea of great magnitude within the North American mind that allows beings in positions of power to manipulate the psyches of those beings in ordinary lives and situations through this indoctrination that the hero is "forced" to use violence. He or she has no other choice but to blow up the enemy.

Much of the information you are fed through these blockbuster movies, is partially financed by agencies that want this concept firmly planted in the minds of ordinary North American beings. We are not conspiracy theorists, as you say in this society, but we are telling you that financial institutions assist in the production of these movies so that the average human is indoctrinated into this form of conflict resolution. Of course, it does not resolve conflict. These concepts increase conflict, but you believe they resolve it. This allows you to be manipulated, and you believe it because you have repeatedly gone to theaters to see this kind of information.

The ego mind is very powerful and very well financed in your society, and we bring this information to you to let you know what you can do to increase the peace, love, and connection in your own lives. You do not associate your divorces with watching blockbuster movies, but there is an association. You will not associate the sickness in your bodies with watching blockbuster movies, but this is an association that is true. If you lower the vibration of your minds by watching violence all the time, your bodies will reflect that lower vibration through the manifestation of physical sickness in your structures. Keep that in mind. When you watch anything, consider it food for your bodies, for your lives. Is this the information you want in physical manifestation? If the answer is an honest no, then do not watch it!

Romance Movies Reinforce the Myth of Love

Another form of fodder for your ego is the romantic movie. Finding that one special person who can solve all the problems you have is a powerful drive in the ego mind. Once again, the ego's favorite game is played through these movies that tout romantic love as the salvation of life, of existence. (Keep in mind that you use the ego mind's desire for violence and judgment in your other movie selections.) You go into relationships seeking salvation in another being, which is what these movies promote. There is one being who is the one who can rescue you from yourself and solve all your problems, but when you are in the ego mind, the one who temporarily relieves your suffering is unable to shift the violence and disease and disaster in your life because that person is not responsible for it or powerful enough to alleviate it. Only you can do that. As the shine wears off those initial romantic encounters, this being is then blamed for all the disaster and destruction in your life — these films feeding, once again, the ego's idea of judgment, separation, and satisfaction with disaster.

Consider what you watch. Do you watch a fictitious concept of romance that is not based in reality? Many movies offer good messages about overcoming difficulties, finding inspiration, and experiencing transformation, and these are the kinds of movies we would like you to watch. Do not feel overwhelmed by our recommendations. We are merely giving information and letting you know why your life is dysfunctional. You have not been told that all these things you do cause and magnify dysfunctions and precipitate your suffering. Your society does not tell you that your pursuit of that one special love will make you sick, but it reinforces the idea of separation, telling you that every being on the planet is unacceptable except for the one being who is your salvation. It also reinforces separation by reinforcing the idea that your salvation is found in another body. It is not found in another body; it is found in knowing the power of your mind, your spiritual nature, and your connection to the nonphysical. That is where your salvation is found.

Choose Entertainment That Supports Growth

The masses who go to violent, blockbuster movies and romantic movies in a desperate attempt to find relief from their lives do not realize that they are perpetuating their difficulties through this idea of separation that is promoted in these films. So when you think about watching a movie, think about the message behind the story. There are restrictions if you wish to wake up, if you wish to connect to the nonphysical, and if you wish to bring peace, harmony, abundance, and creativity into your life in a comprehensive and self-aware fashion. Things will need to be removed. Remember, you are not just removing things from your life; you are also creating space for the Divine, creativity, and peace to enter. It is only in the state of peaceful awareness that knowledge from the nonphysical can be imparted to you. Until you reach a state of peace of mind, you will not comprehend separation and deny its support, let us say, so that you act and do things that do not perpetuate the separation your ego wants. When you reach the state of peace, you can truly take in new information that is not ego driven.

The ego loves war, and it does whatever it can to perpetrate war in all its forms: in families, in bodies, in countries. Not until you are at peace will the ego be in a subdued place and do what it is supposed to do, which is keep your physical body alive — fed and watered and cleaned and housed in the basic forms. That is what the ego is about. If you do not understand it — if you do not comprehend its food and what happens when it gets out of alignment and is given too much energy — you will not be at peace. You will not be able to tap into the spiritual mind, the higher mind.

This information will assist you in making choices that will support your growth, your understanding, and your transformation into the peaceful, spirit-focused being you wish to be. You can create heaven on Earth in this spirit-focused, peaceful place. You tap into forces that are divine, miraculous, and eternal, and you are supplied with everything you need and everything that will benefit you in all ways. This does not mean you will be a poor bag person begging for pennies because you are not focused on the material. That is not the case. Remember that the material comes from the nonphysical; every material possession and every material object in your world is designed by a mind that is focused on experience.

Learn this concept, and apply it to your chosen forms of entertainment. Watch things that inspire you, make you feel good, and bring you understandings that assist you. You will be surprised at how many such things are out there, especially on the Internet. That is where you have a magnificent choice of nutrition for the mind! You do not need to be bored. You can pick whatever subject you are passionate about, whether it is gardening or cooking or politics or UFOs or spiritual philosophy. You can find endless hours of entertainment and information on the Internet that will feed your passion and inspire you to delve deeper into yourself, your creativity, and your mind. This is what we encourage you to do.

Take advantage of available technologies. Delve into the library of information that the human mind has created on this planet. Of course, you have nonphysical transmissions such as channeling that can add to your education and feed that which you wish to increase in your life: love, abundance, creativity, joy, health, and so on. Think about this when you watch a movie. Is it focused on health, or is it focused on death? Is it focused on love, or is it focused on destruction? You will get more of whatever you put into your mind. What you focus on increases, and where you put your energy grows. These are simple truths. This is not an airy-fairy moral judgment; it is about vibration and focus.

Remember, you have at your disposal the most powerful focusing device ever created, and that is the mind of the awakened human being. However, you must understand what you are doing in your society to dampen that energy and to turn off the receiver. We are telling you what you are doing so that you can at least have a free and conscious understanding of the impediments you inadvertently employ in your life that prevent you from tapping into higher mind.

CHAPTER 10

Change Your World by Changing Your Mind

As your eyes focus on your television screens, you think you see the world's political structure, but be warned: It is not as it appears to be. The democracy you believe you live in is no longer that; indeed, it is what you might consider a police state. Most of you who behave yourselves by paying your taxes, going to work, and living ordinary lives in a way that you have been told is correct have no idea what is really going on behind the scenes in your political arenas.

We do not wish to be negative here, but we must be honest. You no longer live in a democracy, and you no longer have the rights you were told you have. Your politicians can come in at any time, particularly in the United States, and do anything they wish with you, and there is nothing you can do to stop it. So when you have the opportunity to look at your voting system and your political structure, understand that you are really powerless within this structure to make any change whatsoever.

There was a time when politicians paid attention to you and were in touch with the constituents they answered to. There are politicians who believe that is still the case, and they are deeply involved in their jobs. They believe that the system still works, but it does not, and you must understand this. You must change your world from the inside out. This is very difficult for the earthbound and materially focused human mind

78 ✳ Spirit of the Western Way

to believe, but it is the truth. The world you think you live in is not what you believe it is.

This world that you live in is a manifestation of a mind — a powerful mind, if you will, the ego mind. It is a mind that believes in separation and war, and that is why the world looks the way it does. As you feed the ego in your Western society with ideas of violence and of a special, highly idealized relationship that will save you from the world and yourselves — bad foods such as mind-numbing television — you are indeed feeding a mind that wishes to make war.

War is the ultimate manifestation of separation, and that is now the focus of your politics. The power structures behind the façade that is presented to you concentrate on war and control. They will usurp your rights if you cross a line and misbehave in any way they deem is dangerous to their agenda. Understand this truth, but do not go into fear. That is what they want you to do, for fear disempowers you, and that is why they propagate terrifying stories on the news. Many of the beings in power are behind the news industry that disseminates what appears, to those who do not know any better, to be truthful information. These beings want to perpetuate your fear. In your fear, you will vote for war. It is that simple. When you are in fear, you feed the ego mind and vote for separation and war. That is the vibration of the mind immersed in the information that comes from the political and military-industrial complex. We are not trying to make your life bad by teaching you the truth; we are trying to get you to focus on shifting your consciousness.

You see on the news programs battles and wars taking place on the other side of the planet, but in your materialistic world, you are not taught that they have anything to do with mind. The outside world you see reflects the inside condition of the collective mind. Your world reflects your minds. Your marriages, your relationships, your work, and your creativity reflect the state of your minds. You are all in a collective dream, and the collective dream is manufacturing violence, pollution, and war. You are immersed in the material mind, the ego mind, and it is only in changing your collective mind that you will begin to shift the collective experience you have in that (what you believe to be) material world.

This material world reflects your energy, focus, and beliefs. Every decision you make in your world, from the foods you buy to the political parties you support, comes from a mind that is based in the material. If that is not the case and you are not focused on the material, you will support companies and activities and beliefs that are out of accord with the ego's desire for war and separation.

Love the Unlovable Projections of Your Mind

When it comes to your politicians, realize that this is not a subject separate from your spiritual practice. The politicians in front of you now represent the state of mind and the state of energy that the collective mind has created and projected. These are words we use to refer to manufacturing, or bringing into existence, certain things. We will define them here a little bit for you.

We use the word "projection," and this means a person is completely unaware that he or she is making an experience. You are innately creative beings, and everything you think about becomes a reality. Everything you focus on with passion becomes a reality, but if you are unaware of that, the experience results in projection. When you encounter objects and events, either global or local, you believe they are outside you. However, you made them happen through your focus, through your fears, and through your thoughts. You are not aware if it, so they seem to be separate; they truly seem to be something that is not of you. This is how we describe projection.

Let's say you have an argument with a family member. In your projecting mind, you think that person is wrong, evil, or bad and deserves your judgment. This is the projecting mind's experience. When you understand that you are the creator of your reality in all of its aspects, you remove some of the unpleasant things from your mind so that you can live in peace. You put those unpleasant things in the outside world. You project them out there, and you think they are gone and you can live in a semblance of feeling somewhat peaceful even though there is underlying guilt and fear lurking in the mind. You see these objects, these events, and these people as outside you, and they appear to be bad. However, these are aspects of you that you decided you could not live with, so you placed them outside yourself. You are unaware of that, and this is projection. You are completely unaware of what you have done.

You are creative beings who are divine, nonphysical, and energetic

80 ✳ Spirit of the Western Way

in nature, and you know that this world is a creation of the ego mind. Such beings can, indeed, extend this creativity from a conscious place. We call this extension. You can love beings who are unlovable because you understand that they are a projection of your mind. The only way to come to a place of true peace and connection to your divine nature is to embrace everything you see, knowing it is a part of your mistaken identity, if you will. The being who is angry with you simply requires love; that will heal the wound. A country that your country appears to be at war with is a fragmented aspect of your collective consciousness, and to stop the war, love is required.

This is not what your politicians tell you. You are told to arm yourselves, to defend yourselves. You are taught to attack to get what you want and to get security. That is not how you get security. You must look back on your history to clearly understand that all the wars — all these projections onto the apparently objective world, all the attacking of bodies and foes — do not do anything. Attacking bodies ruins families, destroys young peoples' health, and kills young beings who believe they are doing the right thing. They are not doing the right thing; they are merely joining in a collective dream that is a nightmare. We want you to exit the nightmare and have a pleasant dream of peace and joy and love, and in our prescriptions and explanations here, you will find the solutions to all your problems.

Take Back Your Power

Your problems are gifts in disguise. Your problems are the solution to your separation from that which you call divine mind. (We do not use the word "God" very often. It upsets people or triggers thoughts that are untrue.) Your connection to divine mind will empower you. It will bring love and joy and health and peace to your planet. What you are (and have been) doing will not. It is very important for you to understand the power you have. You have the power to shift your political structures by changing your mind!

It is within the structures of your mind to practice forgiveness, be nonjudgmental, be kind to yourself, and understand the truth of who you are and what is going on. In this way, you can shift your thoughts about your entire experience — not only the political and military experiences that you witness, but also all of the experiences you have with yourself, your family, and everyone else. Forgiveness must be brought to the forefront of your mind, and peace must rise there before it can rise on the planet. So the political structures that you have made through your overindulgence of the ego are not there to assist you in the way you think anymore because the collective mind has become ego driven and separated from Spirit. Your political structures are also ego driven and separated from Spirit, and only through your shift in consciousness will you have any real effect on your world.

It is very hard for you to imagine how changing your mind will do anything. You think you are one little being, one little speck that cannot make a difference, but trust us, there will be a grassroots revolution. As you all begin to change your minds and shift your focus from war to love, from fear to love, and from separation to communion, there will be a massive shift in energy and focus in your country, and you will have a massive shift in political focus and emphasis.

This is not a mistake! You create the wars you see. You perpetuate the societal powerlessness that has allowed power to amass in the structures you now see at play in the world. Massive corporations, the military-industrial complex, and the pharmaceutical industry are all manifestations of your lack of connection to your personal power. The power seems to amass outside you because that is what you have believed and have been taught. By taking back your connection to Source, your connection to divine mind, you will reconnect with your power, and you will allow it to integrate within your mind. Through that process, you will, indeed, shift the outside manifestations.

Lo and behold, if you all focus on love and forgiveness and you practice the lessons we teach, you will have a miraculous shift in your outside world. You will see it first in your family. Fractious relationships and bitter contentions will disappear. You will see it in your physical body because this is also a manifestation of your separated and confused mind. You will become physically healthier and stronger. As you continue these practices together as a country, as you bring these practices together as a unified demonstration of your dissatisfaction with the status quo, you will manifest a different experience in the physical world. Your politicians will become saner and more reputable. They will be motivated to

82 ✳ Spirit of the Western Way

act in accordance with good and love and health. They will pass legislation that promotes organic foods and that reduces the military-industrial complex's power. They will pass legislation to restrict pollution-creating industries. They will shift their emphasis onto sustaining healthy communities, supporting people who need help finding good employment, and caring for the physical health and well-being of children. These are the changes that will come in your political structures if you begin to change your mind!

Separation Is an Illusion

You must take this on an act of faith initially, for there is nothing in your teachings that proves this will happen, but understand that when you sit down and watch a violent movie, you perpetuate violence in the world. You are all connected. You are all associated in the same mind. You believe you are separate, but this is an illusion. You are not separate. When you revel in a violent movie or a violent video game, you are the very essence of energy that creates war on your physical plane. When you read a book about spiritual evolution and are kinder to your family members (yourself included), you create peace on your planet. These associations must be understood.

Your scientists on the leading edge of developing mathematics and physics computations are discovering this. It is becoming apparent in their brilliant minds that you are all connected and that what you do in one part of the universe affects the other. Yet the ordinary human being such as you does not truly comprehend this because of indoctrination in separation and powerlessness.

This is happening intentionally. Turn your televisions off, and get to know yourself. Read informative and instructive books, and get in touch with your creativity. Reach out to your friends and family, and speak to them about what you envision for your future. Do not depress yourself by listening to war reports on the television. They are not real. The wars and the negativities you see on the screen are the results of confused and lost minds, and the only way you can change them is to begin with yourself, in your thoughts and the immersions you allow.

Turn your politicians off. Vote, if you feel you need to, in alignment with what you have always done or what you believe to be the best, but if your politician stands for war, separation, violence, and judgment, do not vote for that person. Choose somebody else who will have a more peaceful attitude even if that goes against your family or your history. Look at what that has created! Sit down for a moment, and honestly look at the world in existence. Know that war does not solve problems, hatred does not solve problems, and separation does not solve problems.

It is time for a global revolution to align your minds with love and your thoughts with forgiveness and to shift your creative process from the inside out, for it begins on the inside. Your material world is just that — material. It comes from the nonphysical. The nonphysical creates the physical. Your physical wars come from minds that are not at peace. Your pollution comes from science that is separated from Spirit and does not understand the interconnections in the natural world. Your physical sicknesses come from minds that are disconnected from the healing power of love and the divine mind.

Do not expend any more energy on political campaigns. Begin an internal transformation, and seek political leaders who can help you change your world. You will not survive as a species if you continue to vote for the same people you have voted for. It is that simple. They do not have your best interests at heart, and even the local politicians are confused and do not understand what is at play here. Begin the revolution from within. Your politicians are puppets controlled by corporations and beings who do not care about your welfare. You must care about your welfare and that of your families by exhibiting love instead of judgment, care instead of fear and attack. You have the power! This is the most wonderful part of this message: You have the power to create the world that you wish. You do not need these puppet politicians.

You need to change your mind, and you need to get together with other beings who are changing their minds in prayerful and spiritual ways. Come together to focus your attention on that which you want: a world of peace, love, healthy food, clean air and water, kindness, cooperation, and communion. These are things you want, and you must focus on them in your mind. In the short term, find a politician who is the most closely aligned with those goals. There are not many of them out there, but as we disseminate this information and speak about these subjects, more beings will be brave enough to stand up and say, "I will go into politics because I wish to change the world for the better. I wish to clean up the air. I wish to support clean energy. I wish to support peace. I wish to support natural health and uncontaminated foods. I will stand at a podium, and I will ask for your vote because that is what I wish to see!" It requires a groundswell, a grassroots change of mind, and you are the one who can begin it in your world. You are more powerful than you know. You have the ability to shift your planet from the thoughts that you have. Then the thoughts that you have will join the thoughts that other beings have, and you will indeed manifest a system that is in accord with love if that is where your focus lies!

CHAPTER 11

The Fallacies of Western Religious Thought

Many of you are not religious in any way. You see yourselves as secular beings in the material world — perhaps scientists who believe in proof, the evidence you see with your own eyes. Others are closely tied to a church. Perhaps you grew up in a church, or your parents are religious, but you are wavering. You did not find comfort there or the answers to your prayers. You might have seen its ways as narrow-minded and judgmental, and you have decided that you do not really wish to play the game your parents played. Some of you are deeply immersed in religion, and if so, you are very brave to read this book. You express some dissatisfaction with your religion by reading something such as this. Many religions would not encourage reading this kind of material. So if you are in a religious organization, you must have some dissatisfaction with what is going on.

Those of you who are secular and disillusioned about religion have seen the error of some religions' ways. (We are referring to Western society. There are many religions around the world, but we are speaking to the Judeo-Christian society, this Western culture that has been developed based on that religious heritage.) Now, you do not truly realize this as you walk through your secular days without going to church or praying or any such thing, but the entire structure of your society is based on this being you call Christ and the church that has risen from

85

86 ✳ Spirit of the Western Way

his teachings. These churches are not teaching his teachings, but they have risen from them and the stories that have been told about him.

There are many structures in your society that are hidden from your view. They are foundational elements in your society, however, and they affect every single thing you do. We tackle some of these here and describe how it has affected and still affects you.

The Evolution of the Christian Church

There was no Christian church when the one you call Jesus was teaching. He was not trying to create a church; he was trying to create transformation in the minds of suffering beings. It was that simple. He was trying to teach them how to be happy. This is not something many of you think about. You think he established a church that carried on from his teachings, but that was not the case. He merely wanted beings to be happy.

He experienced and understood the causes of suffering, the causes of problems in the mind, and consequently, the causes of problems in the lives of the beings in the time and place in which he lived. He was given divine inspiration and was shown how to assist beings out of the mire of the ego mind, out of violence, and out of oppression. In fact, the oppressors who Jesus was trying to help others overcome usurped his teachings to create those structures. So at that time, the religious structures that existed in Rome — the many gods and goddesses — and the political structures were entwined. There was no separation. Many beings in positions of power saw the effect that this man had on people in his area and in other areas as stories about him were shared and disseminated. They saw that this being had profoundly influenced the populace with his miracles and his teachings of love and forgiveness, and they feared the groundswell of reaction. For political reasons, they decided to take his teachings and to adapt them to their own structures.

They did this with great precision, and they were careful about the teachings they allowed in what became the Roman Catholic Church. They decided to eliminate any teachings that empowered the people, that told them to follow their own guidance, and that told them to live free, creative lives. By getting rid of these teachings, they disconnected beings from some of the most profound elements of what Jesus taught. They did this on purpose because much of what Jesus taught was about personal transformation through direct connection to God, which did not leave any place whatsoever for a power structure. It left no place for a heavily oppressive regime, and it left no place even for political influence. Jesus counseled people to follow their personal inner guidance and to connect with their divine natures so that they could manifest whatever they wanted in their world. This was blasphemous in the sense that it did not allow for an intermediary to influence and wield power over any individual, so it was censored.

This was the energy of the early church. It was not set up to disseminate Jesus's true message; instead, its goal was to keep the authority in place and to influence the populace. You must understand, a revolution of love was under way that was fueled by the miracles Jesus performed, and it greatly influenced beings. The people realized something was happening that they did not understand and that this being had information that they did not have but desperately wanted. Jesus had returned from his journeys in the Far East with information and techniques and skills that had not been experienced yet in that part of the world.

We are going over the early structure of the church so that you are not under any illusions of what it was and is. It is a political power structure, and that is its purpose. The people within the power structure believe they are doing the right thing and are assisting people, but there are higher-ups and internal workings of the system that are very detrimental to the health, well-being, and spiritual evolution of humanity. So we are, indeed, pulling at the foundation of a large structure. That is okay. It is time for this structure to be dismantled and for the truth of your true nature to be revealed.

Let's travel through time to the Middle Ages. The church became very dangerous — a murderous, rampaging monster. Those were the times of the Crusades and the Inquisitions, hundreds of years of death and destruction of wisdom, beauty, and the feminine principle. A rapacious, violent, and bloodthirsty system was at work that had absolutely nothing to do with the teachings of the one you call Christ. Such energy was of the ego mind, and at that time, it was wielded by beings in power who saw the church's influence and went into it not for any kind or religious or spiritual teaching purpose but to hold power and influence and to get what they wanted.

88 ✳ Spirit of the Western Way

This went on for many, many centuries, and the devastation that the church wreaked on the world was horrendous. People were burned and tortured for no reason other than expressing spiritual views that the church did not approve of. Many, many women were murdered for practicing the natural crafts of healing and midwifery. Much wisdom and understanding was lost from the world because of the misteachings of this structure.

Expressing any kind of connection to the spirit world or spirit guides became life threatening, a matter of life and death. Parents counseled their children not to explore those arenas for their own safety. They did it out of love and protection, so children were punished when they referred to spiritual connection in any way, shape, or form. They were punished when they explored in the woods or played with the spirits that lived there. They were punished when they spoke about their dreams in any meaningful way, and those dreams were dismissed as meaningless.

For centuries, humans have repeated this scenario, and it has become deeply ingrained in your culture, this idea that venturing into the non-physical world is unsafe. You have been told that there are demons and negative energies there and that it is the devil's playground. You have been told that the only way you can, indeed, come into contact with divine mind is through the church's structures and the church's instruction. These are the beliefs you have now in your society.

We review this history because these points are the foundation of your culture. You do not realize it. You think your modern culture is separate from this spiritual Christian business, but it is not. The religious structures that exist in your country are limiting. They are based on untruth, and they are based on a history of violence and oppression. They are based on the teaching that Jesus is the only son of God, a divine being who is different and separate from you. That is not the case. He was indeed divine, but you are divine too. You are an aspect of divine mind manifesting on this plane to experience itself and understand itself, so you are given this opportunity to understand yourself by creating a world that reflects what you are.

Each of you has a world that reflects what you are on the inside. Your fears, the family you are in, the work you do, and the body you reside in are all physical manifestations of what is going on inside your mind. The religious structures that exist in your society are physical manifestations of what has gone on inside your mind, which includes restriction, limitation, and fear of the nonphysical.

You are a divine being who has come here to investigate and understand and experience all of the beliefs that you have — good, bad, and indifferent — and that is what you see around you. That is what you see in your wars, your sicknesses, your loves, and your joys. But the religious structures as they exist at this time, the Christian church as it exists at this time, are out of alignment with truth and will not take you to the place you seek. They insist that you believe things that are not true and that you act in a way that is out of alignment with your truth.

Reject Sacrifice, Martyrdom, and Suffering

The ideas that you must sacrifice yourself in this life to reach heaven is a lie that will lead you down a path of extreme suffering. When you pass from this world, you will understand that you were taught things that are not true.

We are here to assist in unraveling your society's long journey into fear. We do not judge anything that Jesus did; he was a divine teacher, a wonderful prophet, a being who is with us now and whom we are working with to finally bring out the truth. This channel speaks with Jesus, and he is here again to convey his messages about what he taught and what his life meant. It was not what the church teaches.

The church teaches about forgiveness, but it is the ego's definition of forgiveness: Sin is real, and it needs to be punished in some way by God or in hell or through some such fabrication. The only hell is the one you create and live in in the mind. When you are out of alignment with truth, you create a hell. It is designed that way so that you feel bad when you remove yourself from truth. This gives you a contrast so that you can understand what is going on. But the teachings of the Christian church, as you understand them, are confusing this issue, and they tell you that suffering and sacrifice are good.

These are based on erroneous explanations of what Jesus's life meant. He did not sacrifice himself in the crucifixion; he demonstrated the timelessness and the nonmaterial nature of his body. He came back in a new body and continued teaching for many years on the Earth plane. He

90 ✳ Spirit of the Western Way

demonstrated his abilities and the truth of your abilities: When you are fully aligned with truth and fully divine, you are not limited by the physical. This is what he taught. At any time, he could have removed the threat to his life, but he did not need to. He understood his capabilities, and he understood the message that needed to be disseminated.

Jesus's message was distorted by the structures we referred to earlier. They decided to make him special, to separate him from ordinary beings so that they would not believe in their ability to transform themselves and their lives. This allowed the powerful to continue to have power and influence over people, and this has continued throughout history and into the present. You have been disempowered by these old structures that now seem to be fading from the forefront, but your culture still clings to the idea that connection to the nonphysical is bad, that you will suffer, and that the devil plays in that playground. Many movies and stories in modern society perpetuate this untruth.

Explore Your Personal Connection with God

There are lower energies that can access you if you are in a low-vibrational state, this is true, but we are speaking about raising your vibration. We are speaking about focusing on a spiritual connection to divine mind and using your guidance system for its true purpose, which is to show you when you are off track. Our purpose here is to free you from the oppression of the church and the psychological prison you are in and to give you back your freedom and ability to manifest your dreams and your reality.

Before those of you who are in the church abandon your faith, educate yourselves in the truth of Jesus's teachings and investigate the discoveries that are made about the documents that were edited from the Bible. We do not want you to abandon your faith at all. We want you to educate yourselves on the history of the church and read books about its foundational days. Read books about the editing of gospels that were, indeed, intended to be part of the teaching. Educate yourselves on the history and the brutality of the church, and understand that it had nothing to do with God, nothing to do with Jesus. Through that investigation, you will be able to put your current perceptions in perspective. You will see that there are misteachings and that you have been deceived.

The pastor who stands in front of you in church on Sundays is not a

The Fallacies of Western Religious Thought ✳ 91

deceiver; he or she is most likely a very honest teacher, but this history of deception and distortion has caused much suffering in your society, and it is time for it to end. It is time for you to take an internal journey to explore your personal connection to God. You do not need an intermediary; it is not designed that way. Jesus will come to you in your prayers, and he will come to you in your seeing mind. You will be able to develop a relationship with him that is personal, intimate, empowering, and helpful in understanding your divine nature and your tremendous ability to create in your world.

You are not separate from God in any real sense even though you feel as if you are because of the misteachings of your society. You suffer because of those misunderstandings. It is time for you to understand the true nature of your self and the one you call Jesus. And it is time for you to understand the true and misleading nature of the Christian church in modern society.

Stand Up for Yourselves

The vagaries and vicissitudes of your society cause you much confusion, and this is why we go into these subjects so carefully. You have hundreds of subjects in your society that give you pause, that take you down a garden path but do not lead you where you want to go. However, we do not want to be negative. We have told you about many things that are wrong with your society and why some things that you do bring you down, but now we want to bring you up. We want you to focus on what you can do to bring forth the kinds of experiences you want to have, the kind of society and personal health you want to create. We have given you many, many examples of where you are off track, and now we want to give you some direct guidance on how to be healthier and happier.

The first subject is mind training. This is something many of you have been nervous about. We always refer to *A Course in Miracles*, and the lessons contained within it are one of the quickest ways to wake up. They teach you to act against the ego's thought system. You repeatedly choose love, and you let things go that the ego wants to judge. The book asks you to align with forgiveness and love and compassion, and its frequency helps you. Many of you resist this particular text. The reading can be difficult because of the Christian language (as you perceive it to be) and the resentments you have with that language. Understand that these resentments are part of the block you have to your spiritual evolution.

Everything done in God's name that is violent on your world is a lie in terms of its association with Spirit. Anything that the church has done that inflicts pain on children or restricts people's freedoms or punishes anybody or constrains anybody's creativity or self-expression (we could go on and on) is, in fact, blasphemy! That is why these words bring up such limiting ideas in your mind: It is what has been done with them rather than the truth of the essence and energy behind them.

The fundamental structure of your society is poisonous. It has been infected with fear, control, and at times, perversion. You have built a society on these building blocks, these bricks, and your society is teetering. It is addicted to these thought structures because they have been so powerfully and violently pushed on you for millennia. We must address the particular distortion that the church has a place in the modern, new society that is coming into being. The truth is it does not.

Align with Love

In the form it is in now, the church has no place in this new society because it has been built on fear, cruelty, repression, control, and sexism. None are building blocks you want to take into the new world. These are many of the reasons your world looks the way it does right now. What would the world look like without the church? Many countries are fundamentally aligned with the Catholic Church, and they suffer from the diseases of mind that this particular institution has fostered, fear being the most important one. Fear of death, fear of retribution by a cruel God, fear of hell — these are all ideas in the minds of those beings who follow the Roman Catholic Church, and they corrode the world. They keep the global frequency down.

These are fundamental structures of the collective consciousness, and they allow crime after crime to be committed around the planet because of the frequency they set. Remember, things of like frequency band together, so when you have millions upon millions of people believing in hell or that they are going to go to hell, believing in the sin of the flesh, believing in Satan, believing in evil, and believing in a punitive God, these powerful collective thought structures will continue to create like frequencies. The revolution that is imperative at this time calls for you to align yourselves with love rather than the church. This is important for every one of you to understand, especially those of you who have children and feel in your hearts that something has been amiss in the church's structure — its history, behavior, and tenants. You are right! There have been many ills perpetrated on this planet by this particular organization through the oppression of people who worship at its feet.

Stand up, brush off your knees, and defend yourselves by loving yourselves. We ask you to stand up for yourselves by declaring,

> "I will no longer do things I don't want to do. I will no longer hurt others — children and family and friends — by carrying on a tradition that is poisonous and has caused so much pain around the world. I will take only the good from the church — its teachings about kindness, its teachings about helping others — and nothing that is to the detriment of myself. I will look after myself. I will make myself healthy. I will become fearless, I will let go of my unloving ideas about myself and reality, and I will become strong in the alignment that I now stand firm with — love."

Make a dedication today to align with love, truly and absolutely. That means to stand firm in your belief in loving yourself and in your belief and commitment to your powerful ability to create. And we want you to align with forgiveness. This means you do not attack the church. Do not curse it or try to bring it down through any act of violence or aggression. Look after yourselves and begin to love yourselves and trust in your inner guidance because your inner guidance is aligned with that blueprint that is your destiny.

Each of you who is a revolutionary in this wonderful transformation of your society might feel intense conflict. We ask you to side with love against all odds. We ask you to side with fairness and with a healthy sense of self against all odds because your society is founded on the opposite because the church has terrorized people into believing in those principles.

94 ✳ Spirit of the Western Way

You all must take a true look at what has been created by the church — the sadness, the repression, and the control — and see the effect it is having and has had on your world. It is a purveyor of violence and hatred, and it has singularly caused many of the problems now playing out in your world: the world of violence, the world of war, the world of judgment, the world of prejudice, the world of persecution, and the world of sexism.

These are all firmly footed in the church, and it is time to have this conversation out in the open so that you can express your fear and your outrage not only at the church but also at what we are saying. You have been indoctrinated, and if you believe in it, these words will upset you. They will make you angry, but you must understand the truth of what has been done in Jesus's name, in God's name. This world would not look the way it does if Jesus's teachings had been followed to the T. He taught about self-expression, creativity, and the disciplined and loving training of the mind that is required to bring your tremendous creative powers into being.

It is time for you to accept that you have been given the creative force of a god and that it has been used against you. It is time for you to begin to discipline your mind toward love because only the mind aligned with love will create a loving society. You must put down your arms, your judgments, your prejudices, and your fears, and you must stand firm in love. It is only in love that you will step out of this dark age into a new golden age, and it is only in standing firmly and with absolute conviction next to your brothers and sisters and aligning yourself with equality, peace, and nonviolence that you will shift the actions you see in the world.

This is collective reality, and those of you who have bought in the fearmongering and the stories of hell and damnation contribute to the war. You do not know it because your frequency is low. You are scared and limited and feeling fearful, and these are the essences of war, the low frequencies that produce fear and create violence. You must step up from these low-frequency thoughts into the new, higher frequency that will generate the new world we are all here to help create.

Be brave. All of you who are terrified of the church and of your mothers because they have been dogging you with their religious beliefs must stand firm, and with love, say,

The Fallacies of Western Religious Thought ✳ 95

"I am no longer willing to cower in the darkness of this behemoth, the church. I will stand in the light of love, arms open, defenseless, and willing to be counted."

This will upset many of you who go to church and believe in the church, and that is okay. It is time for these words to be spoken. It must come to pass that these old structures built on suffering, sacrifice, death, and destruction are brought to their knees not through any violent act but just by walking away and saying,

"I will no longer support these structures. They do not bring us what we need. We must band together, all creeds, all colors, all nations, men and women both. We must band together and stand firmly on the side of love and refuse to participate in any limiting or dogmatic thinking that separates us from one another as people, as countries, and as religions. It is time to step into unity consciousness, and it must be done in this incarnation. It must be done as a group, it must be done as a united front, and it must be done now!"

There is no time left to think about this. There is no time left to wonder what will happen. You see your world crumbling, and you see the violence perpetrated by the way religious fanatics look at the world. You must see the world as a united front. You must see your brothers and sisters as exactly that — your brothers and sisters. You must let go of the old before the new can grow. We are here to teach you how to do it, encourage you to do it, and insist that you do it. You do not want to go down the road you are going down, dear ones. You have been on that dark road long enough. Step toward light and love. Let go of the guns, the hatred, and the prejudices, and step into this new world with us. You will, indeed, be amazed.

CHAPTER 12

Everything Is Connected

Science arose in the mind many centuries ago as a way of observing the world. From that observation, facts were discerned about the planets, plants, animals, and these kinds of things. Scientific exploration of the world began many, many eons ago as humans observed empirical evidence and analyzed it every day. They gathered information from their observations of events and actualities. For example, they determined that seasons had repeating patterns.

As science developed, humans became confused about their observations and began to layer religious beliefs over them. There was a time in your history when scientific observation was contaminated with religious doctrine and dogma and things were forbidden, in a sense. You were not allowed to question the age of Earth, and you were not allowed to question the divinity of creation. This caused problems. Eventually, science was separated from religious dogma, and at that time, it was a very important event. You must understand that the limitations placed on scientific observation by dogma, superstition, narrow-mindedness, and an absolute belief in a punishing God who would attack you if you should question him limited people's ability to see and understand.

This separation occurred in the late 1800s, beginning with Darwin's revelations about evolution and natural selection. The proposition that creation was continuing was blasphemous. It became quite a contentious issue, and a necessary path of scientific exploration began. It was necessary to separate empirical evidence from the creationist view. It allowed humans to see that creation was still under way, that things were evolving, that systems were not static, and that shifts in materiality were happening. The idea that a creator God performed only once became archaic.

However, in that separation, limitation and segregation developed that has proven detrimental. The absolute removal of this idea of a creating force, an animating force that is divine in some way, from scientific inquiry resulted in a system that is quite dangerous, and this is what you are experiencing now. The scientific method eliminates the most profound aspect of divine mind, and consequently, systems are being designed that do not take into account the whole. Scientists do not take into account the consequences of certain actions as they are undertaken.

For example, this method has led you to develop pesticides that kill insects and harm your food supply. The pesticides cause more harm than the original problem, and this is a result of segregated thinking. It originates from considering systems as separate when they are not. Everything is connected to every other thing. This is a spiritual principle that must be reintegrated in your scientific method.

You see, your scientists who do not have this spiritual principle underlying their designs and experiments believe they can contain one system and manipulate and change elements within that system without any consequences down the line when, in fact, each effort goes out like ripples from a stone thrown into a calm pond. All your actions have consequences, and all the manufactured aspects of your life cause effects. Now you are feeling the consequences of the removal of spirituality from science, and it is time to reintegrate that aspect of spirituality — not dogma or religion, but spirituality, this idea of oneness — into the scientific method. It is truth; it is not something that is up for debate. Everything is connected, and your scientists are now proving this.

Allow the Oneness of Energy

The systems that have developed on your planet as a result of ignorance, separation, and segregation are causing a great number of problems. This can be seen in prescription drugs designed to act on one part of the body and have consequences on other parts that are just as detrimental as the original disease. Because these systems are driven by profit and not sanity or spiritual principle, the pharmaceutical industry has no qualms in offering up a drug that is quite detrimental to the holistic being. Profits are overriding sense because of the separation of spirituality from science.

You see this in food production in which genetically modified crops are drenched in pesticides. This is insanity, and you are reaping the rewards of this insanity, of this isolated-system belief structure that ignores the consequences to other beings. The bottom line is that money and profits drive these activities, and you are paying a tremendous price for it because spirituality and values of a holistic nature have been removed from the decision-making process.

You are at a point in time when it is very important for spirituality to be integrated into every aspect of your life because you have reached a very powerful position. You are engineering things in the biological, chemical, and environmental realms that are beyond your ability to understand. You allow scientists and governments to do things that are detrimental to the whole. This will not be allowed to continue. This is not a threat of any kind; it is merely a natural consequence.

You see, your natural environment, your world, this consciousness called Gaia, is indeed an individual being. Your Sun is a being, just as Gaia and your other planets are beings. You are not taught this in your society. You are taught that these objects have no life to them, as far as you are concerned. As far as you are concerned, these beings are of no specific consequence in your mind's eye. This is a very detrimental view of things. In fact, your Gaia is a very intelligent, creative, nurturing being, and she offers up her body for self-expression. She offers up her body as a supplier of foods and wonderful natural environments in which other beings can reside. You have disrespected her tremendously through lack of understanding and ignorance of the systems that are at play. Now is the time for you to correct this. Now is the time for you to understand this.

There is evidence coming into your world now, and ironically enough, it is from the scientists who are experiencing physical demonstrations of the connectivity of everything. They are learning this from a mathematical and scientific point of view. To keep science separate from spirituality now is indeed ignorant. It is old and archaic thinking, Spirituality must be reintegrated in a nondenominational, nonreligious sense so that there is no single discipline but rather an understanding that there is a prime cause, if you will. There is an energy that vibrates through the universe and animates everything. It is the motivating factor in the principle of life expressing itself. It is this factor, this unknown energy, that pervades everything. By not allowing this oneness of energy to come into the equation, scientists ignore the most powerful principle at play. You cannot say that scientists are intelligent in ignoring this factor. It is very narrow-minded and dogmatic in its own way. Science has become as narrow in vision as the original religious thoughts it separated from.

It is time for scientists to remove these blinders, this fear-filled idea that if you bring spirituality into science, it will limit it somehow. This is the opposite of what would actually happen. If you bring spirituality into science, you will expand your results and your influence and you will receive information from the nonphysical that will assist you in solving the problems you have created through this narrow view of things.

Integrate Science and Spirituality

The experiments that show the connectivity between atoms that are far from each other demonstrate the connectivity of everything, including the connectivity of thought manifesting in the environment. As you change one aspect of thought, you change another; it is all connected. So when you change one human mind on your plane, all minds are affected. This brings to mind the saying, "If you wish to see change in the world, change your mind about the world," which is a principle of A Course in Miracles. You are indeed creating the world from your thoughts. Scientists create the results of their experiments from their narrow-minded beliefs. By expanding their belief systems, they will observe different results from their experiments and come to a more profound understanding of what is beneficial for humanity and the planet.

Your planet suffers from this separation from nature, this separation from divine manifestation that is life expressed on your planet. You cannot tamper with one aspect of life in a closed system because there is no such thing. Everything is connected, and if you come at science from a materialistic point of view only, you will have very limited and damaging results. You are experiencing the consequences of science separated from spirituality and from wisdom.

Wisdom is not something you can live without. You need wisdom in your actions to understand and to create the correct result. Wisdom is knowing that you are all connected and that conditions cannot be separated from actions. Scientists have acted on principle, believing that a system is isolated so that they can, for example, design a chemical that kills plants but nothing else. But of course, there are myriad animals that live on those plants, and they also die. Those animals live in different environments, not just that one environment in which that chemical is used, so another environment is disrupted and brought out of balance. The human lack of balance — lack of awareness in designing chemical systems and experiments and about the consequences they produce — causes these problems in your society.

That is the reason science must be reevaluated and spiritual principles must be brought into the scientific method. You will see the world holistically, and you will not cause damage in one system without regard for the consequences from that decision. You will see that when you pollute the air, you breathe that same air into your bodies and pollute yourselves. All the systems on your planet rely on water to thrive, so you can see that when you poison water, you poison your entire planet. These are the things that you must realize, but as long as science and spirituality are separated, you will not be able to heal the wounds that you are inflicting at this time.

Adopt a Holistic Approach to Life

We are reeducating humankind so that you understand you are not individual physical specimens living on a planet that has no consciousness, isolated from all other beings, born into physical bodies that you leave, and that is that! This is as far from the truth as you can get, and it is time that we brought this subject out into the open. You are an eternal spiritual being. You temporarily dip into materiality to experience and to come to an understanding of certain aspects of your physical manifestations and your abilities and skills. You return again to the nonphysical very quickly, in relative terms, dipping in and out as long as you feel you need to and as long as there is misunderstanding.

We are here to eliminate the misunderstandings, and one of them is your scientific method. That method no longer serves you. The scientific

102 ✳ Spirit of the Western Way

method that is currently employed allows you to kill each other, invent monstrous weapons of mass destruction, and pollute your most beautiful and luscious environment. Now is the time to step into a new belief system that gives you some kind of responsibility for caring for this wonderful planet. It is time to take responsibility for passing along an environment to your children's children that is clean and can be used. And it is time to view the body holistically.

It is time to view the body as the magnificent system that it is. Stop treating it as separate organs with no connection to each other. Treat the entire person — body, mind, and spirit — rather than just individual sections that you believe to be solely material. That is fiction. It is not scientific at all. It is clear that mind affects body and that all of these systems work in concert. To isolate a particular chemical, to isolate a particular system, and to manufacture drugs that affect one particular thing without any thought to the rest of the being is ridiculous and quite ignorant. The holistic nature of the human is ignored, and you must bring body, mind, spirit — intellect, heart, and passion — into all your activities, to be healthy and of sound mind.

This holistic nature must be implemented in all your systems. Governmental systems ignore the reality of what humanity, education, and cultural evolution are, which make up a fruitful and creative life experience. These are all separations that have happened as a consequence of separating spirituality from science. It has become an epidemic in your culture. You have become a truly secular society in your beliefs, but that does not mean you are material beings. It does not mean you are only logical beings, only intellectual beings. Just because you believe it does not make it so. You ignore the most important aspect of your life on Earth: You are all connected. You are all of one mind, and you are mistaken in your belief about separation. The mistaken belief in separation causes many of your problems.

It is time to approach this belief with intelligence and love and awareness and to bring back to the scientific method the understanding that the mind influences everything, and when you observe and design an experiment, you bring your beliefs and influence to that environment. There is no objective reality whatsoever.

You always, always influence the experiments you conduct, and that must be understood, discussed, and contemplated in the scientific world. You have become so influential over your environment and each other that it is time now to reintegrate spirituality. We do not mean religiosity or dogma. These are things we want you to dismantle. What we wish you to come into contact with, what we wish you to reintegrate into your lives, is your connection to the Divine and to the nonphysical as they speak to you. This is a private and personal matter, but it must be taken into consideration when designing experiments. It must be taken into consideration when designing educational and food-production systems. These have all become separated from Spirit because of the belief that spirituality is negative and obscures objectivity. However, the objectivity that arose from this artificial split has caused more problems than it has solved.

CHAPTER 13

Experience True Wealth and Freedom

One of the great benefits of your society is your ability to choose, and this is what we seek to enhance. Understand that when we tell you to unplug your television sets, we are not doing it so that you will have nothing to do or to inflict pain on you. We do it because that is an important way to reclaim your freedom of choice.

We have frequently spoken about your society's conditioning programs and how they work. Understand that they work because they infringe on your ability to choose. This is how your society has been manipulated by those who understand that when you do not use your free will and your creative self-expression, they can control you. Each moment of every day — each second — you make a choice. Whether you look on something with hatred or love is a choice that creates. You are indoctrinated in judgment, fear, and the belief that the body is your salvation, and these belief systems contaminate your ability to create the world that you want to create.

The world that is out there right now — the warmongering world, the environmentally devastated world, the world of financial and sexual inequality — has been exploited and manufactured by high-level operatives (we will call them) who have a very, very deep and clear understanding of human creative potential. They have used your energy to supply themselves with influential, powerful, and lucrative systems.

106 ✳ Spirit of the Western Way

The world is not going to hell in a hand basket for no reason. It is going because you as a collective do not understand the power of your thoughts and your minds. You do not understand that the choices you make in this moment affect everything. Do not dwell on the negativity we bring to your attention. We do not want you to hang out there, but we must let you know what has been done and is still being done to your collective consciousness through these systematic conditioning programs that pervade your person-to-person behavior. This is important for you to understand so that you can shift your consciousness, moment by moment, as the influencer you will come to see yourself as being.

Invest in Your Life

When you go into financial fear, for example, you empower the financial system that is at play, and this financial system is not designed by you or for your benefit. It is designed by beings who want to skim off all the wealth of your society and keep it for themselves to use for all kinds of reasons we won't go into at this point. When you go into financial fear, you shut down and worry and worry and worry about your money. You empower the thought structures that others have been feeding you when they ask you to invest decade after decade, century after century.

Why do you think these powerful systems ask you to give them your money? They do it to keep you in a state of intense fear. It used to be the church that took money from beings who had very little. For centuries, the immense wealth of the church came from people it intimidated and scared, but as you came into the twentieth century, the church began to lose its power. That is when the banking system emerged; thus the savings and loans and mortgage systems emerged, and they now take your money. So do not think that these systems are separate and new to your world; they are not. They have been here for a very, very long time, and that is why we keep repeating our message that you have been taken down the garden path. We want you to see that keeping your money is a very important part of this world's evolution.

What do we mean by "keeping your money"? We mean use the wealth you generate through your jobs and through your creativity. Perhaps you are an artist, and you sell paintings. Perhaps you are a photographer, and you work at weddings. Putting that money into the economic system so that you never get to use it is not saving it. It is losing it. You have been taught that to have massive savings means you are wealthy. No, it does not! We want you to use your money to enhance your life instead of putting it away for a rainy day in a banking system that cannot give it back to you.

If you all went to the bank today and asked for your money, it would not be there! It never will be there. They are using it for other things. They convince you to hand over your hard-earned cash on a promise and a prayer, and they will not give it to you if you ask for it all back. Yes, there would be a few of you, the first ones in line, who would get something out, but trust us, most of you who have great savings accounts would not be able to get it out if you all went at the same time. This means it is not there. The system is based on fabrications, on lies.

Invest in your life. If you drive a gasoline-powered car and you have money in your savings account, take the money out, and buy yourself an electric car or a more environmentally sound car than the one you have as a demonstration of your love for the planet. If you have money in the bank but you buy cheap or unhealthy foods when you go to the grocery store, invest that money in your health. Buy organic and humanely produced foods. Use your money to enhance your life in this moment! If you have money in the bank and you have neighbors around you who are suffering or family and friends who are going without, use that money to give them something they need, such as a new pair of shoes or a new outfit for school. This is how money should be used, and you will realize the benefit of your wealth in the moment.

As you get closer and closer to this new world, the old system will fail, and those of you who have a lot of money tied up in investments will not be able to access it, so we are giving you the heads-up here. You cannot postpone your creativity. When you take the money you earn and put it in a safety deposit box or some such thing that the bank has told you will keep it safe, you do not realize the energy you create. You shut down the feedback system that says, "I am wealthy." You look at numbers on a bank account screen and say, "I am wealthy," but you do not feel it. You do not experience it, and you do not truly express it because it is a mental concept. The wealth you have been trained to experience by this artificially symbolic system of money is only a mental construct, and as you feed

108 ✳ Spirit of the Western Way

into it, you have a mental experience that is not true wealth. True wealth is seeing the benefit your hard-earned cash can bring into your life. Put solar panels on your house, and step away from the grid. Give your children a beautiful experience they will remember forever. These are real demonstrations of wealth that we encourage you to participate in.

Of course, you have been indoctrinated in debt as part of the financial system, and you must attend to it. Debt is a prison, the hell of the modern financial institution, and you must realize that buying a new car and going into debt is not a benefit when you have money in the bank. This is what many of you do. You pay interest on money you do not need to borrow, and you do not live the life you truly can afford to live because the banking system, the monetary system, the fear-driven slave-money system, has convinced you that you should not spend your money; you should give it to someone else who will look after it for you. They are not doing that.

Support Businesses and Organizations You Believe In

If you have a lot of money, understand this: Invest in tangible benefits to the world, yourself, and your children. Be healthy. Be kind and generous to those around you. Help systems that need financial assistance, such as underfunded systems, alternative health systems, and alternative schools, for example. If you have a substantial amount of money sitting in a bank and you believe the education system is less than ideal, invest in a local alternative school. Seek systems that require financial assistance, and invest in those.

Building companies that head toward the new world can be very, very sound financial investments. Take your money out of the old system, the old companies that are destroying Gaia, raping the world, and stealing the funds of the honest and the sincere participants in this cocreative project, and use it to benefit that which you believe in, that which you want more of, and that which you know is benevolent. That will be whatever you are attracted to. It could be art, food, science, technology, or health care. It does not matter where you place your funds in terms of experience. You don't have to give your money away. You can invest in sound environmental businesses that really need seed money to get off the ground.

We want you to understand that true wealth is experiencing, in this moment, what you have invested in, what you have put your hard-earned time and effort into. We want you to understand that money kept in a bank account that you see on a screen once in a while is not real wealth, and we want you to know that it is not going to stay there.

Begin to work through your beliefs about money and your financial fear, and see where you have been indoctrinated by the banking system. Those banks look very impressive — big granite pillars and big stairways — because they use psychology to get you to believe that they are safe, epic, and substantial in nature, but behind that façade is a gambling, dishonest, and disrespectful system of thievery. The reason you have financial fear and you grasp and hold on to this money is that you have been trained to do that.

Think about the animals of the field, the birds, the fish, and all natural organisms. They live in the moment and access the wealth of their environment through their present experiences. Many of you do not live full lives. You have been trained to postpone it until retirement, postpone it for a rainy day. Use your wonderful resources of creativity, community, and generosity, which are wonderful qualities, and you will begin to reap rewards immediately. You will begin to see the benefits of this changing way of financial interdependence.

Align with Nature's Generosity

The system will break, and we make no bones about that. The system has been drained by the upper echelons of greedy and manipulative banking and by financial cartels, so it is just a matter of time before you lose it. Realize it! Put that beautiful addition on your home. Pay your mortgage down so that you own your house, and change your heating and electrical systems over to solar power. Put a water collection system on your house so that you are not dependent on a tap that somebody else is in control of. These are things you can do to realize the wealth that is truly yours. Put a beautiful garden in your yard, and invest in nutritious soil for the plants and the food and the flowers you want to grow. Allow your grandchildren to have a wonderful camping experience.

Stop putting it in the banks, stop waiting for a rainy day, and stop waiting for that moment when you will be safe from the world. You will never be safe from the world when you live in financial fear; you will only be safe from the world when you understand your tremendous creative power and influence. We are trying to bring that message to you in many ways, but you are the ones who must make the choices. You are the ones who empower these old systems.

You are in the driver's seat, but somebody else has the controls of the car. Just like a driving instructor's car, you are given the illusion of control, but you really don't have it. Educate yourself about these archaic, manipulative systems that do not bring joy, which is one way you know they are not love based or healthy for you. When you think about the money system, debt, and banks, you generally do not feel that great unless you are in the higher echelons and understand how it all works.

If you have a lot of money and have figured out how to use the system, stand firm in love. Use your money to assist your brothers and sisters on this planet. Hoarding to feel safe is one of the most unloving systems and beliefs that your society holds. It is self-centered and selfish. Look at it. Do not just shut this book and say, "My money is my money, and I will never give it to anyone." Just look at the system that is at play, and understand that this is a tremendously wealthy planet. It is wealthy because of the natural resources that Mother Nature gives you: the air and the trees and the food that grows beautifully in the soil. All you have to do is plant a seed. That is wealth and generosity.

We want you to align yourself with these natural systems. Watch the birds and the bees, and see that nature does not hold herself back for a payment. Begin to see yourself as part of nature's system, part of a generous, ever-expanding, creative, and loving system that can feed all of you very well. Stop voting for warmongering politicians and acting from a place of financial fear, and start being truly generous and loving to yourself by eating well and nurturing your body and mind with loving and healthful elements. Then, when you feel really good, look around your world, and ask, "Where can I help? Where can I be of assistance?" You are a Westerner, and you have the most magnificent opportunity to be generous! Feel your wealth by sharing it and by investing in truth, love, and kind systems that will last and bring your Earth into this new and wonderful chapter of her life.

CHAPTER 14

Stop Judging the Body

There are many detours in your society that steered you away from the direct road to love and into the brambles and the boggy, mucky ditches of fear and judgment and confusion. Each chapter of this book is significant in that each area of your life can take you into fear and, frequency-wise, down from the higher levels we seek to help you reach.

Earlier, we described how the body is created and how it gets sick. In terms of your society's treatment of the body, we want to point you toward shifting that. You are trained to intensely believe in and worship the body. Women, in particular, have been indoctrinated in valuing themselves solely on their physical structure, how pretty or beautiful they are, and even certain body parts are emphasized. A particular set of assets, breasts, is offered up as a gift to a sexual partner, resulting in feedback that could be very detrimental to a woman's belief about herself.

Most of you in the modern world have been deeply indoctrinated into valuing the body. Even if you were born many decades ago, you were raised in a sexist society that promoted beauty, whether that involved thinness or curviness. It does not matter which quality is proposed because either is a quality of physicality used to designate your value. This is increasing for men now as the mass media focuses on six-packs and muscles and so on, but they have a lot more leeway in terms of how they are perceived. Their value is not directly associated with

112 ✳ Spirit of the Western Way

their bodies. Some men use their bodies to get attention and build their perceived value, but it is a much more common problem for women because it is a patriarchal society, and the patriarchy has set the standard for value. Men are given more freedom and more value in all ways, financially and physically, and their work is valued even if it does not require anything more than brute strength. Men who do menial tasks are paid much more than women who do menial tasks. There is also a double standard when it comes to people in the public eye, such as television personalities or performers. Men do not have to conform to the same rigid beauty rules as women do.

These issues reduce the frequency of your population. Women are very judgmental of each other because they have been taught that such behavior is acceptable. Of course, we are not physical in nature, but many of us have lived in physical bodies. We look at the energy that is lost from judging the body, from hating the body, or from loving the body and worshiping the body. None of these thought systems works for your frequency, and we are concerned about that. We are concerned about frequency. How you lower it is really irrelevant in terms of moral or value judgment. We do not care why you lower your frequency, but we want you to know that it is not serving you as a person or as a society.

So every time you look in the mirror — male or female, it doesn't matter — and attack yourself as not being beautiful or handsome enough, tall enough, muscular enough, or thin enough (it does not matter), you are being unloving to yourself. You are attacking your society and causing suffering not only in your mind but also in the collective consciousness. Because you feel bad, you hurt your psyche. Your psyche generates and creates in your life, so your contribution to the collective is negatively affected. Because you believe your body is separate from others and that your thoughts are private, you think what you do is harmless. You do not understand the laws of creation. When you attack your body, when you say you are not acceptable because your nose is two millimeters off center or is too big or too small, you destroy the ability to bring positive outcomes into manifestation. We are referring to self-loathing and this kind of thing.

The other side of the coin is the person who constantly perfects the body to gain positive attention. You might think this is harmless. "If I love my body and it looks beautiful and I am appreciated by other beings, then this is a good thing." Well, it is not such a good thing. If it makes you feel good in the short term, it can benefit short-term frequency-raising behavior. However, if it is a physical structure that will change over time — let us say your face or your body, it does not matter (obviously time takes its toll on the human physical structure in the conditions you find yourself now) — then trying to perfect it also brings in fear and control issues, demonstrations of fear. It will even bring in a fear of aging, of being less than you are now. So in the short term, you might look in the mirror and say, "Yes, I am beautiful in this moment; therefore I am valuable," but it will undermine your ability to align with your true nature, which is not physical. It is creative, loving, and self-expressive.

Your Body Is a Vehicle

In the nonphysical realms, you play, rejoice, and explore what you bring into manifestation for an interesting life. If you are obsessed with the physical body, either negatively or positively, the mind is kept in a low-frequency state because the physical material world is the effect, the end result, and the lowest vibrational frequency that you encounter. When you are up in the realm of imagination, you are in the realm of your true nature: love, abundance, creativity, and health. But when you are down in the realms of the heavy physical material world, the aging world — the time-based world, the fear-based world, the death-based world thought system — you will feel negative, fearful, and contracted, not expressive, loving, and open. Even though these beautiful bodies temporarily give you a currency of some sort, it is a very temporary and low frequency.

See the body as a vehicle for you to use to explore your consciousness rather than an end in and of itself. Stop focusing on the body, and focus on eating healthy foods so that your body is nourished. Focus on healthy activities that you enjoy — not slogging up hills to lose weight, but going on a beautiful gentle hike in the woods with your camera, perhaps creating a beautiful set of images that you can do something with or simply enjoy for the creative process. See your body as the vehicle that allows you to paint or sing or dance. Do not see it as the value in and of itself. It is not an end; it is a means, the way that you experience your consciousness. If

114 ✳ Spirit of the Western Way

you have a body that is less than ideal in terms of this society's design and value system, then begin to focus on these other areas to the exclusion of your body.

You are not your body. The body is not of God. The ego, separated consciousness, created the body to demonstrate your belief in separation. When you focus on the body, you demonstrate your belief in separation, and you will begin to feel bad. If you use your body to take yourself through your environment, have conversations with beings who interest you, express ideas that come into the mind through writing or painting or dancing, and see beautiful things, allowing appreciation of this most magnificent physical experience that you are having, you will stop suffering in the body. As soon as the ego mind starts thinking about aging or the decrepitude that creeps up on the bodies of low-frequency beings, then you will start to feel bad. You will start to feel fear and panic, your frequency will go down, and you will eat bad foods. The frequency of good and healthy food is higher, and you will not be attracted to them, which will cause a detrimental effect on the body.

Beings who are obsessed with the body might have eating disorders or intense hatred of the body, or they might demonstrate a need to control the body. This is the ego mind focusing on the body to the exclusion of everything else. Many of you focus on the body too much because of your training. So if you are a woman who struggles with beliefs about the body, focus on the positive experiences that this body allows you to have. Focus on being able to go for a walk on a beautiful summer morning. You will be able to listen to the birds or see the sunrise. These are ways to use the body to bring you joy rather than the detrimental negative feelings of worrying what you look like in your shorts simply because you have been indoctrinated to do that.

This indoctrination, this valuing of the female form for currency, is part of the patriarchal structure in which men wield more power. As you step into more powerful realms as a woman, this contamination goes with you, so even though you might have a doctoral degree in philosophy (very intelligent and well educated), you are still going to be judged on how you look more than a man with equivalent qualifications will be judged. You must not join in that game.

Focus on Activities That Bring Happiness

Step aside from focusing on your body as your value. We are not saying don't brush your hair or your teeth or wear decent clothes. Wear what you like and what's appropriate for the profession that you have chosen, but focus on your creativity, conversations, the energy of communion, and your passions, and the body will fall away from your conscious judgments. It will take care of itself because these other areas are high frequency. Creativity is a very high frequency. If you are immersed in painting, dancing, writing, or gardening, the body just takes its natural place in your experience.

So if you suffer from negative frequencies generated by hateful thoughts about the body, refocus the mind on that which interests you, that which causes curiosity or passion to arise in your body-mind complex, and train your mind from focusing on the physical structure as the end or the means to an end. Understand that your mind and spirit will bring you that which causes you to have a fulfilling and exciting life.

We hope this helps to clarify the body-worshiping situation in your society. This does not mean you should not exercise your body; it means that you should focus on that which you love and that which interests you. This will create activity in the body-mind complex that is a naturally rising energy that will say, "Take me on a walk. Take me for a swim. Let's go up that mountain to see what's on the other side." This naturally rising impetus comes from the mind that is occupied with things it loves. So if you struggle with your body, your weight, or your physical health, focus on what you love.

Listen to the inspirations that come as you become happier and happier and more and more focused on your passion, your creativity, and loving the world as it is rather than hating and judging it and doing the same with your body. These things go together. When you love the world, when you love people, and when you bring to the table that which you believe in, your body will naturally respond in a healthy way. These unhealthy, judgmental thoughts attack the world and the body and cause you to turn inward in a hateful way, attacking this physical structure that is designed only to take you on a journey through your consciousness.

CHAPTER 15

Transform Your Destiny

Your society is transitioning from a dark, patriarchal, fear-laden and fear-driven society into a new era. You must be willing to step into some unfamiliar territory so that the new society can develop. When you look back at your history, you can see the death, destruction, fear, and limiting ideas and beliefs that are laid out in the form of oppressive regimes and strict social programming that do not allow you to flourish as spiritual beings. You must say, "I do not want to carry on in that tradition. The tradition of my ancestors is not what I want to repeat here." Otherwise, you will stay on the same trajectory of war and death and destruction and environmental devastation.

You must face your conditioned thoughts and beliefs and ideas about being different because that is really what stops you from changing the world in which you live. You do not want to stand out. You do not want to upset the apple cart. Perhaps you do not want to upset your mother or your traditional way of looking at the world, but you must be willing to shift and change, or you will not be able to create a new society. These are fundamental issues you have: You fear being seen, you fear being different, and you fear you won't fit in.

This society is not happening to you as a victim; this society is created by you as a member of a collective, and the powers that be know they have trained you well. They have trained you to understand that standing

118 ✳ Spirit of the Western Way

up in a classroom and making a mistake brings ridicule, and they have trained you to ridicule each other. You must develop the internal ability to ignore this conditioning on your journey through and out of this limiting thought structure that is the Western way.

Make the Effort to Shift

When you are trained the way you have been trained in your society, deeply indoctrinated in fear the way you are, a great effort must be put in by the part of your mind that is connected to Spirit, by the part of your mind that knows it is suffering and does not want to continue suffering. A great deal of effort must be put into undoing the conditioning you have been a victim of, and this is why *A Course in Miracles* is so important. It goes deep into the psychology of the collective consciousness through the individual consciousness that is yours and shifts it at a fundamental level, turning your mind from fear and judgment to love and acceptance. This is what must happen for you to shift your creative frequency.

If you are immersed in fear and worry and judgment and separation, you emit a frequency that is very low, and you will manifest low-frequency systems, activities, thoughts, words, and deeds. When you are in that low frequency manifesting these negative experiences, it is hard to be happy, to feel good, to be inspired, and to do those things that we ask you to do here. In fact, it is impossible because the things we ask you to do are high-frequency, loving, self-nurturing, and creative activities. All these things hold a high frequency, and if you are immersed in the ordinary Western-conditioned mind that has watched war movies and violence decade after decade and has been raised in the education system and in families that offer very little love (dysfunctional socializing and these sorts of things), then you are not going to be able to make the choices we are asking you to make.

We must point you toward documents and texts that will shift your frequency so that you can make new decisions. These new decisions must arise in a different kind of mind, in a mind that is already stepping away from the mass destruction that this society leads you toward. This society has trained you in war, consumerism, and behaviors that cause many problems, and it is not going to change because it works for the structures of coordination and organization that have put these systems into place. It works for them. You give them your money through the banking system, and you are taught to be quiet and compliant. You do not express your feelings because of your social, family, and religious conditioning. You are like a flock of sheep being led over a cliff, and you do not have any ability to step out of the crowd unless you do something with your psychology. Be willing to entertain the idea that there are things you don't know.

This is the first step in the decision-making process that we ask you to contemplate. Look around at your world — your healthcare systems, your education systems, and your warmongering military-industrial complex. You will see that these systems cannot go on, yet you all participate in them. We ask you to entertain the idea that what you are doing is not in your best interest. If you can entertain that idea, then we can get you to move up in frequency just a little to be willing to look at a document that will help you understand what has happened, what is happening, and why you must change the way you look at the world.

To truly shift your consciousness — to go deep into the basement of your mind and to recalibrate this amazing creative device you have been given — be willing to look at the lessons of *A Course In Miracles* as a daily practice that will completely and absolutely shift your consciousness in one year. This is very, very quick. For the ego mind that wants to shift its consciousness in one minute by having a drink or turning on a television show, a year sounds like a long time, but that year will pass regardless of whether you shift your consciousness or change anything. If you change nothing in that year, you will continue to manifest low-frequency experiences, and you will continue to feed the machine of the Western world, which is leading you into oblivion.

Do this work as a demonstration of your love for humanity — your children, your grandchildren, and your fellow brothers and sisters who travel on this planet with you. We know we are asking you to do something very big, but it is the only way you will shift enough minds to stop this train that is heading over an environmental-disaster precipice that will cost you a lot in the long run.

Yes, we ask you to be disciplined. Yes, we ask you to act as if you are a member of a giant community because you *are* a member of a giant community, a community that has been led in ignorance into dangerous waters. We are here to help you understand that you have the key to your freedom in your mind and in your heart. That is where it lies. It does not lie in the world of high finance or banking or in the beautiful bodies that you all strive for. It lies within your heart and mind. You must understand how the heart and mind work, and that is what we are here to encourage you to do. When you study your mind, you will see that fear and judgment and hatred make you feel bad. You shouldn't do those things because feeling bad is not nice!

Feeling bad is your inner guidance system telling you that you are off track and mistaken in your thinking. The inner guidance system has been given to you as a gift of love from the Divine, or God, if you will. It is always in alignment with love, and if you step out of alignment with love, you will feel bad, lost, separated, and depressed. These are the feedback mechanisms you have been given to tell you when you are wrong and causing suffering.

When you change your thinking, you change how you feel. To change your thinking, you must excavate and remove from the mind beliefs that are not in alignment with love. You must go into your mind and change it before you can change the world, which is your life, and your life with everybody else's life is the collective destiny of your planet.

CHAPTER 16

Use Technology to Inspire Others

Technology is one of the great purveyors of ego in your society, but it is not all bad. We don't want you to give up your portable devices (phones tablets, laptops, and so on). It would be foolish to ask you to give them up completely, but we want you to know that there are many detrimental programs filtering through your computer systems. The programming that comes through your phones (which are portable computers) is quite detrimental to your health. They disrupt your electromagnetic systems, and your cellular structure struggles to maintain health when these technologies are constantly in use. Put down your phone. Put it in your bag, and put it in airplane mode so that you don't miss your calls and you are not always engaged with it.

The mind that is constantly fed information and constantly distracted the second it feels uncomfortable is a mind that will not evolve, and this is a part of technology that we are concerned about. When you have a negative feeling, a slight dip in emotion, most of you reach for this new soother — your phone device. Your phone device distracts you from that dip in your mood, so you never address what is going on with your feelings. You reach for the soother as soon as you are upset. It is no different from the parent who constantly puts a pacifier in a baby's mouth, essentially training that child to stop expressing him- or herself.

Put Your Phone Away

Remember that Spirit uses your feelings to guide you. When you are off track, your guidance system dips a little because you have had some unloving or hateful thoughts or ideas. You override the guidance system by immediately seeking a distraction to bring you out of that negative thought. Now, in the short term, you will feel a little better, and that will help your frequency. However, in the long term, you will not grow, and you will not see how your mind affects your feelings. How your mind affects your feelings is how your mind affects your life!

When you have a hateful or negative thought and you immediately reach for your phone or computer, you find distractions that are low frequency, and you strengthen that frequency. If you feel a dip in your mood and have the self-awareness and training from the practices that we suggest, you will see that you have stepped off the path, and you will inquire, "What did I just think that made me feel bad? Oh, I had a negative thought about my body. Let me repair that. Let me appreciate the body as the vehicle that it is, and let me send some loving thoughts to the part of my body that is causing me difficulty or the part of my physicality that I am judging negatively." Then you will raise yourself out of that frequency into a higher frequency, and you will feel better. You will resolve something permanently!

When you go into your mind with awareness and the training we suggest, you can filter out the thoughts and beliefs that you do not want to encourage. When you are hooked into your technology all the time, you constantly reinforce the ego's thought system. That is what these devices do. Unless you are in awareness and specifically seek spiritual material to watch, study, or listen to, you will be fed the program of the modern Western world. You will feel worse over time, and your frequency will go down because the powers that be, the marketers, and the system builders are not high-frequency beings, and they do not have your overall best interests at heart. They want you to consume, to purchase, and to be in fear because when you are in fear, you purchase more, and you become a better consumer. Good fearful beings are consumers because their consciousnesses are focused in the physical material world. That is where fear keeps you.

Spread Beauty Through Technology

Use your phones for what they are designed to do. Use them to take some photographs of beautiful things. That is a wonderful thing to do! Post these images of life on your Facebook pages. If you'd like to share inspiring and uplifting material, do that so that you are sending love out into the ethers rather than consuming fear. For most of the day, leave the phone down. Never walk around with it in your hand, and when you are at lunch with your friends, put it away so that it is out of your sight, and shut the ringer off so messages are received but you can live the life in front of you. This is where you lose ground, evolutionarily speaking.

You are constantly, as a group, away from the present moment when you can shift your consciousness. The present moment is when love is expressed. The present moment is when you learn to interpret your guidance system and train it to focus on that which is good, that which is loving, and that which you want more of. These are simple practices, but they are very powerful compared to the low frequency of the anxiety-inducing practice of constantly seeking information that you do not need.

This world is a reflection of you, and these technologies reflect the collective mind in the frequency that it holds at this time. That frequency is not high. We are not judgmental or offering a detrimental view. Look at the world and what you are doing to it — the wars and the fears and the scarcity and the violence — and you will see that there is a low-frequency vibration happening here. These products accentuate and promote that frequency. They thrive on it, so you must use them with caution. You can use them for good. Think about food, for example. It can be abused and used to hide your true feelings, or it can nurture and nourish and help and heal. These devices are the same. You must have a high-frequency intention when using them.

These are the ways we want you to use these devices. Unplug them when you don't need them. Put them away when you are engaged in daily life, and understand that they hold a frequency of the Western way. The Western way is what we counsel against.

See your addiction to these devices. For those of you who work with them daily, this will be a challenge, but you can train your mind to see them as tools rather than the life's breath that keeps you going. They are not your life's breath; they could all be gone tomorrow. There are no

124 ✳ Spirit of the Western Way

guarantees that these devices will always be here, so think about that. What would your life look like without them? Step back a little from your habits and from your constant need for them. They are like candy, and as you know, it is not good for your body-mind complex to eat candy all the time. It is not good for your spiritual evolution to be hooked into your devices all the time. They can be used for good, such as to heal and to spread the word of love.

So make sure that you step on the right side of the fence and that you use technology to disperse messages of love and inspiration. Do not use it to spread fear, to warmonger or attack each other, to gossip, or to inflict pain on others. When you post a violent or aggressive video or Facebook message, you attack other people. Low-frequency emissions infect others, and high-frequency emissions heal them. It is that simple. So do not post negative things; post positive, inspiring, heart-opening, and love-inspiring things, and you will be using these devices appropriately. Employ them with a conscious and aware mind that knows what it is up to.

CHAPTER 17

Create Space for the Divine

Integrating these messages into your life is one of the most difficult things for the heavily conditioned mind because it is overwhelmingly urged from within, from the training that it has received, to continue on in the familiar way. This is the difficulty most spiritual practitioners and students have in your society, and it is because the conditioning is so powerful, so deeply entrenched, and so repetitive that it is arduous to change, especially when the beings who surround you are conditioned in the same way and are being pushed by the same seemingly unchangeable thoughts, words, and voices.

For example, you might be sitting with friends at a party, and you say, "I feel really bad that I do not earn enough." The being next to you feels exactly the same way and says, "I suffer from the same thing. I don't think I'm successful enough." You are both expressing the voice of conditioning that has been instilled in you through education, your parents, and the media. You think and feel there is something wrong with you for not earning more money because other people feel the same way.

You are not going to get feedback from the world that supports your new direction. You are not going to hear support from others unless you move yourself to a spiritual community of some kind. If you live in the ordinary Western way, you will not hear these revolutionary ideas from other people. If you learn something new and share it with people who

126 ✳ Spirit of the Western Way

are not on the same path, you will be shot down. You will be told that you are wearing rose-colored glasses, that reality is tough, and that you must knuckle down and do what the world requires of you. This is the reflection you will get back because it is what you believe at this moment.

When unpleasant feelings arise because you believe such thoughts, you see them reflected in the world. Your beliefs are reflected back to you, and that is why the training programs in your society are so effective. Once a person is trained to believe a particular belief over and over again, it will manifest. When you believe you do not earn enough money, you create a world in which you need to earn more.

You change this belief by knowing that this is going on. The world reflects your collective minds, and these collective minds have all been trained to believe in money, work hard, be ambitious, see success as only financial, and so on. You are swimming in a sea of conditioning, and that sea will not give feedback that is different from the information you have all put into it. Your constant beliefs reinforce these visions and experiences.

As you begin to change your mind, you must put some effort into reconditioning it. If you want to change your beliefs, you must have a systematic and repetitive reprogramming system to assist you with that, but it is very difficult for the dysfunctional mind to reprogram itself. It can be done, but it is a difficult job when you are constantly reconditioned in your conversations, work, and recreational activities.

First, turn off your televisions. It is the biggest indoctrinator in your society, and it is intentionally hypnotic. (We won't go into a long diatribe about television. We know you know how we feel about it.) You will feel fear that if you don't watch television, you will not know what to talk about. You will not have anything to relate to your family and friends and coworkers, and you will look like the odd one out. One of the big conditionings of your school system is that you should not be the odd one out. We are circling around a little bit here, reiterating some points that we made earlier, but it is very important to understand that you are constantly being barraged by this programing system — from your friends, your family, and your coworkers — when you are trying to change your mind.

As you begin to entertain new ideas about spirituality, you will feel as if you are alone for a while. It is good to join groups and Facebook pages and live-streaming events hosted by spiritual practitioners if you can to connect with like-minded others. You can connect with other beings who are on the same path and can offer you some support as they go through their journeys. You can offer some support in return. You must work to find people of like mind, whether in real time in your community or in an online community where you can make new friends.

These relationships might feel a little awkward at first. You don't know who these people are. You might meet them at a seminar or workshop or something similar. It is important for you to make efforts to commune with beings of like mind. As you change your frequency and your mind and step out of the belief in money and the body as gods and move toward spiritual practices and read your lessons and transform the projections that bring this all into manifestation, you will experience new relationships. You will bump into people who share the same philosophy. You will gaze on a class of similar philosophy and feel the urge to go to it.

Do not take it too seriously when some old relationships and old habits fall away from you. You will change your life because you are changing your mind. This is a very, very fearful place initially for most new spiritual seekers because they are involved in relationships with people they have known for years and years. They feel that if they don't participate in normal conversation, they will be alone, abandoned, out in the wilderness. There is a transition period when you seem to not identify with the old belief system, yet you have not quite made the connections in the new belief system. Be patient with yourselves, and understand that this is a process.

Imagine a very overweight person who is constantly going out to eat and drink with friends. When that person decides to no longer maintain that body weight and to change, he or she cannot continue with the old habits if he or she wants to transform the physical. That is what you are doing. You are choosing to transform the physical by transforming the projection that creates the physical, which is your personal consciousness and your collective consciousness.

As you read this book, there are thousands of other beings reading this very page, and they think they are individual minds too. You are not alone. There are millions upon millions of beings at this time transforming

128 ✳ Spirit of the Western Way

their minds through lessons, meditations, and other practices such as affirmations. You are part of this grass-roots revolution that will manifest a new world; however, as a human being, you must find your way through this transition process. You must understand that the person who wants to lose weight and used to eat out all the time will have to choose salads or, in some cases, break that pattern and choose different activities. You might very well have to choose different activities as well.

Find Activities That Reinforce Change

Turn off your television. That will show you when you need to occupy yourself with something else. If you are an avid television watcher and our instruction to shut it off irritates you or makes you feel as if you will lose your whole life because you feel lonely when you turn off the television, then turn it off in increments. Turn it off for an hour "here"; turn it off for an hour "there." Make sure you don't watch the news before bed, and don't watch the news when you come home from work, when you are tired and need to be nurtured. Do this carefully, and understand that you will slowly find things that will fill up the time.

If you shut the TV off cold turkey, you will have withdrawal symptoms. If you know that it is coming and are willing to experience that, good for you! Do it, but make sure you have healthy activities planned for that time when you would normally be watching television. Invite a friend to go walking with you, read a good book, or take an evening class once a week so that you do not isolate yourself. These are things you can do to strengthen your connection with yourself.

It is important to change your thoughts, the internal workings of your mind, but it is also important to support the internal changes you make with actions that reinforce rather than contradict. Do your best to understand this process. We in the nonphysical are offering as much support as we can to those of you who are stepping away from the old way. You can search for people of like mind on your computers and in your communities, and we advise you to do that. You will find great joy in the expanding and enriching process this journey into love takes you. It will strengthen your relationships and your health, and it will allow you to live longer and more freely. It will align you with your true purpose. It will do many, many things.

The transition period can be a little confusing, and if you feel lonely or scared, it is okay to watch a movie or a show you used to watch as a comfort to soothe you. Don't do it as a habit, but understand that there is a process of relinquishing the old and creating space for the Divine. That is what that empty space is: It is a place where the Divine and love are going to flow. You must create that empty space, so allow those empty feelings to surface, allow that afternoon when you don't quite know what to do with yourself to happen. See whether you can be at peace with it. See whether you can get through it with prayer and meditation and walking and these kinds of things.

The space must be created first for Spirit to come in, so allow that. Monitor your thoughts. Notice when you attack yourself for being stupid or for joining this spiritual practice. Listen to those thoughts that tell you that you will be alone forever if you do this, that nobody will love you. These are the hateful thoughts that you have been conditioned to believe, and they are not the truth! You will know they are not the truth because they will make you feel really bad. It is very good to see them and hear them. Write them down, and explore those beliefs. Ask yourself where they come from, who taught them to you, and why you are so scared to be quiet and peaceful. You will see that it comes from your societal programing that is deeply entrenched in the mind, and that is why we say you must dedicate some time to the reconditioning of your mind. You must allow the process to go through your consciousness gently and calmly without scaring yourself too much.

Don't believe those hateful and negative thoughts, and don't worry that when you have an afternoon where nothing seems to be happening, your life is going to end. It is not going to end. You are merely creating space for Spirit, inspiration, ideas, and some quiet time. Western society does not take enough quiet time, and as soon as they feel uncomfortable, most beings look for something to do. They reach for their phones or their computers or their friends. Reaching out to friends is good, as long as they provide support rather than stress on your new path.

CHAPTER 18

Secrets Do Not Serve You

Many of you have been on what you think of as a spiritual path for many years, yet you have sicknesses in the body, financial problems, or relationship issues that never seem to go away, and you have become quite frustrated. You say, "I have been on a spiritual path for a long time, and nothing seems to be changing." We want to bring to light here the idea of the social face, the face of innocence — the idea that a presentation is offered to the world that is your conditioned self — and you offer that conditioned self to yourself as well.

You put on some nice clothes in the morning, you shower and do your hair nicely, and you put forth a very respectable and acceptable presentation to the world as you head out to your daily activities. If your mind is preoccupied with your resentment for a relative or the fact that you don't like your body, then yes, you have dressed it up nicely. But you hate "this" part and "that" part, and "this" part aches and is very negative. You don't like it, and you wish it would go away. If the social face you present is not a match to the interior journey you experience, your emotional journey, then you will receive very confusing feedback from the world. You will get a frequency reflection of that confusion, the resentment, and those dark, unloving, self-loathing thoughts even though you present a polished and acceptable exterior.

You try hard, do the best you can, and do everything you were taught

131

132 ✳ Spirit of the Western Way

to do to be a good person. You read the right books, try to think the right thoughts, and perhaps have some mantras or affirmations that go through your mind, yet these other things lurk beneath the surface. These lurking things are powerful. These fears and judgments are powerful because those are the things you don't want people to see. They are the things you are ashamed of, the things that scare you, and the things you try to control. What happens for many of you is you exert a level of control for a while. Your behavior, that thing that you present to the world, is done through will, an insisting kind of feeling. It is not a relaxed feeling. It is an "I can do this. I must step up to the plate here. I must do this. I must. I must. I should. I could. I would" feeling.

Inside you is a different being. Inside you is somebody who is perhaps frightened or resentful. Inside you is somebody who is perhaps hungry. There are many, many things inside you that are not expressed. Generally, when you exert control over your behavior for a certain period of time, you can do it for a while, but eventually it crumbles. This is demonstrated by the person who restricts food all the time by force of will and then loses control and binges, buying some donuts or some chips and going home alone to eat them. The person stuffs him- or herself and then feels sick. What is happening is that the person must look at a side of the personality that is not being fed and is being controlled. Something inside that person expresses itself through the binging behavior.

Another example of its expression is the very health-conscious and very well-behaved person who goes to the gym, walks in the mountains, and pays attention to personal care, but in a moment of upset or anger, he or she buys a bottle of alcohol and overdrinks and feels terrible the next day. Something inside that person lets loose and expresses itself.

Have Compassion for Others and Yourself

Now, each of you has your thing that you do in private, whether it is eating food, drinking alcohol, or binge-watching television shows, for example. All are aspects of you that may not be the you that you show others. They might not be parts of you that you are proud of. They might not be parts that you can love and accept. You hide them because they are your dirty little secrets. These are real parts of you, the dark parts of you, or the ideas you have that are untrue, fearful, self-deprecating, or unloving.

These manifest in your life. Just because you don't show them to anybody or express them at the dinner table does not mean they do not create.

This is a very important part of this conversation. It relates to your social conditioning, to this social face that you present to the world, and the real you that is underneath comes out in relationships. You fall in love with the social face, and you fall in love with the person who goes on dates with you and behaves. After a little while of living together, you see this dark underbelly, this part that you did not really see before (although, there probably were clues). Generally speaking, you do not see the truth about someone until you live in his or her home.

Know that this is okay. In fact, when you are heavily conditioned the way you are, some of these dark, secret behaviors are the most illuminating experiences you have. You are conditioned to behave yourself perfectly, and you manage to pull it off all day out in the world. People see you as what you present to them, yet there is this other part that comes up occasionally in perhaps less-than-tasteful cravings or habits or addictions. What you see is the darkness in your mind manifesting in behavior that you cannot always control. This is a gift, and we want you to become much more forgiving and loving of yourselves.

When you give up controlling your food, let us say, and you binge on something that is unhealthy, you see an aspect of your self asking to be looked at. This part of your self asks you to look at it. Is it your loneliness, your rage, or your fear? What is manifesting that behavior?

For many of you, the behavior will come intermittently. It might show up once a month or once a week, and you hate yourself in the morning. You judge yourself and say, "Oh, I can't believe I did that again! That is terrible. I will never do it again!" That is the lament of the morning after. You need to look at this. This is the thing that creates those seemingly negative aspects of experience that confuse you. Here you are trying your best and working your hardest, yet negative things keep happening to you. Why? Because these dark secrets lurk inside your unconscious mind.

Now, they are not totally unconscious. They can come to the surface, just like that, when somebody says something you don't like or you have a thought that makes you feel lonely or unlovable. So they are not unconscious in that sense, but they are not at play all the time, as far as you are aware, because you do not see them. That does not mean they're not creating; they are creating! They are lower-frequency aspects of your consciousness that are always there, being controlled, and they rise to the surface once in a while. The fact that they are controlled does not mean that they are not creating all the time.

Look at those negative, addictive, shameful behaviors that pop up once in a while. You all have parts of yourselves that you do not want others to see. Look at them. See them as controlled, limiting thoughts that have to be expressed once in a while. No matter how antisocial they are, no matter how problematic they are, they must get out. It is like a pressure cooker: Only so much pressure can build before it explodes.

Once you have gone through one of these "shameful" episodes (we use quotation marks because there is no need for shame; it is merely an unloving thought in your head that is expressed so that you can see it), remember that this is what experience is for. It is to show you what you believe. So when your behavior deteriorates to one of these demonstrations of unlovingness, know that you learn and you get to know your consciousness through what you experience.

One of the great untruths of your society is that the face you present to the world is the one that matters. In terms of creation, the feelings inside of you are what matter. They create everything, and that is why you have disparate reflections coming back from a seemingly perfect social face. Negative things happen — sicknesses, divorces, infidelities, or addictions — and you cannot comprehend them because they seem so contradictory to the social face, the face of innocence you present to the world. Let us tell you this: It does not matter what you present to the world. What goes on in your heart, your mind, and your feelings is mirrored back to you in the form of physical manifestation. If those thoughts, feelings, and beliefs are constantly entertained and are creating, then they will create in the physical world.

There are no sins here. God does not look down on you and say, "Ah, you binge drink every Friday night, so you are a bad person." No. Look at what causes you to binge drink every Friday night. Why do you need to numb yourself? Why do you need to do such an unpleasant thing to yourself and your physical structure? What is it in your life that requires this release of pressure? What are you doing, moment by moment, that is not easy and is not in alignment with your true self? That is what causes

Secrets Do Not Serve You ✳ 135

these kinds of things. Be much more loving to yourself when you look at these (what you call) negative or antisocial behaviors.

Take the same approach when you see those behaviors in other people. If you are out on a Friday night picking up some groceries and you see somebody drunk on the street, know that that person is just suffering from an untrue idea, an unloving idea that hurts so much that he or she had to numb it with a lot of alcohol. Look on that person with loving eyes, and forgive that behavior. That person knows not what he or she is doing. The person behaves that way because he or she cannot stand the suffering any more.

The same thing happens with homeless people or others who struggle in a way you do not. They have thoughts, ideas, or beliefs that manifest in the physical world and demonstrate their lack of alignment with love, so what they need is love. This does not mean that you live with them. It does not mean that you even have to help them in a physical sense, but look on them with loving and forgiving eyes, and know that they do the best they can with the beliefs they have. You are the same!

You all have behaviors you do not want anyone to know about. You have secret thoughts and fantasies, and that is okay. Look at them with loving eyes, and ask them what message they are giving to you. What is the message these reflections are asking you to pay attention to? If you don't pay attention to them, they will just get louder, so don't ignore them. Look at your shameful or negative behaviors, and ask yourself what is expressing itself. Is it anger, fear, shame, or loneliness? What are you expressing in these behaviors? You want to know.

Lower-frequency thought creates in your life, your body, and your relationships, and it will not go away. It is what these incarnations are for. Each incarnation you have is an opportunity to find out what these lower-frequency, unloving beliefs are and to bring them into awareness, accept them, forgive them, and (eventually) love them. That is the process, and this is the basis for all spiritual evolution. What are you afraid of? What are you blocking? What do you resent? Bring it to the surface. Admit that it is there, and then forgive it and love it. It takes a while, and there are many of these things in your minds, but know that there is no judgment on this side for whatever it is that you are confused about. It is merely an error in thinking, and it can be changed.

136 ✳ Spirit of the Western Way

See these behaviors as mistakes, errors in thinking that can be changed, and ask Spirit to help you change them so that you can be at peace — true, integrated, and absolute peace. That is where knowledge resides. In that frequency (once you are at peace), you can get in touch with the truth of your nature, of your reality, and you will be able to have direct, conscious contact with beings of higher consciousness. That is where we are. We are in the realms of peace and knowledge and love, and we are trying to get you to step toward them. We cannot make you do it. All we can tell you is that your suffering is an arrow that points toward your errors, and our job is to encourage you and to assist you in whatever way we can in clarifying your minds so that you are in alignment with peace and love.

CHAPTER 19

You Are Magnificent

Millions of people out there feel the same way you feel. Millions are calling Spirit, and they have their work cut out for them in terms of transforming their inner worlds so that they can bring a new outer world into manifestation.

Many of the principles we teach are repeated. We must reiterate these principles so that you get them. You are trained to read books and then put them aside and read more books. What you are doing is tapping into another consciousness that temporarily brings you relief from your worried and troubled mind. These books are different. These books are to be reread, and the advice is to be contemplated seriously, not dismissed out of hand.

Some of you might read these books and say, "Well, no. I am not going to stop watching television. That's a ridiculous thing. How does anyone live in this world without television? They must be wrong. I must be excluded from this prescription." However, if you do not follow our prescription, you will continue to create along the lines that you have been creating for the past few hundred years, and you can see how that goes: wars, global diseases, pestilence, cancer, and so on.

The egoic consciousness tells you that what it wants is best for you and what Spirit wants is worse for you. Why does it do this? What is the conflict that is constantly expressed and experienced in the human life on this planet Earth? The constant battle is between love and fear. Now, you have heard this, but what we want you to understand is that you literally created your world in fear. You hid yourself in this unconsciousness in fear of retribution from the god you believe will punish you. Your profound terror that you will be attacked by the being you believe is God has pushed you to the limit, and relinquishing that fear will heal your mind. This is the most difficult part for you as intellectually trained Westerners educated in the material, secular world.

You do not realize that underlying much of your fear and anxiety and intangible guilt that you often feel is a terror of God. This fear of God was planted early on in your society by the church, and it is always there. It is a belief in death, a belief in the inevitable sickness and aging of the body. These are tangible demonstrations of your fear of God.

If God is love, then how can these things happen? If you believe that this world was created by God and that your body was created by God, then you cannot believe God is love. A God that is loving would not create death and destruction and war and disease in the way you experience it. Examine this fundamental aspect of your mind. This belief in death and sickness shows you that whatever made this place, whatever made your body, and whatever made this world is out of alignment with love. You know, in some part of your mind, that if this is the only reality you have or the most prominent reality you experience, then God cannot be trusted. You made this place. It is riddled with your fears and anxieties and misperceptions, and that is why it is so difficult to live there.

Now, you have disguised this terrorized mind in a world that, at times, can be very beautiful, but if you look at how most of you live — you fear sickness, you fear death, you suffer from financial anxiety, and you have difficult relationships — you might find a few here and there who are peaceful for a while, but unless you have landed on a spiritual practice that helps you understand what is happening, you have a pretty difficult time of it, and, you have an increasingly difficult time of it as you age and head toward that thing that you think is inevitable, that physical and at times traumatic death.

Your Consciousness Is Reality

When we speak about reality, we speak about your eternal nature. We speak about your deathless quality, which is consciousness. Your consciousness existed before your birth. Your consciousness experiences this incarnation and creates, taking in all the information that is at play, and it continues on after you let the physical body go. To really appreciate this incarnation, to really milk it for what it can bring you, you must focus on spirit. The body will take care of itself. The body is the result of what you think about, what you feel, and what you believe is true. As you can see, your body, if you believe in death, will die. If you focus on sickness, which is what most of you do when you are trying to be healthy — you try to avoid sickness rather than focus on vitality and self-expression and energy — how can you increase energy and happiness? You are trying to dodge that bullet of sickness and death.

Through your focus, you can change everything. Through your focus, you can be inspired. "Inspired" means you are in spirit. Focusing on the nonphysical aspects of your consciousness brings you what you want. The nonphysical aspects include creativity, love, and self-expression in whatever form they take. You tend to think of creativity as painting and writing and these kinds of things, but your creativity is your expression of life force. You might want to be a mother, a gardener, a singer, a therapist. It does not matter. Your passion draws you in a particular direction, and that is where your creative genius expresses. If you follow that good feeling — that passion, that positive energy, that curiosity, that interest, that desire to connect with something (be it a person, place, or thing) — that is love expressing itself through you. That is life expressing itself through you, and it is never-ending. You will always have more and more and more curiosity, more and more and more creativity, and more and more and more self-expression if you allow yourself to follow them. That is the most difficult thing for you to do in this society because of your conditioned beliefs about feeling good and trusting in life and love.

So this is how you make yourself healthy and long-lived. Of course, as you make yourself healthier and longer-lived, your death process becomes easier and easier. Eventually, as you raise your frequency into the realms of love and pure self-expression and self-appreciation, your death process will become a much easier thing. Resistance, fear, grasping onto the physical material world, and judgments cause this heavy, dark experience of death and sickness that you have. The lack of love in your mind and heart causes these physical manifestations in your body that lead to traumatic exits from the planet.

You do not have to exit an incarnation in a difficult, violent, or aggressive way. You can simply pass out of this experience into the next experience when you are aligned with truth. This means that in your incarnation, you focus on the truth of what you are. You are an eternal spiritual being connected to Source, and you have access to all kinds of creative inspiration from the nonphysical. You have the ability to directly communicate with us in the nonphysical. There are layers upon layers of consciousness above you that are joyful and loving and self-expressive and unified. These are the beliefs and the thoughts we want you to entertain as you retrain yourself because the mind refocuses from judgment and fear and death to love and light.

That is what the lessons of *A Course in Miracles* are designed to do. From those lessons, you will see the negativities in your mind that you are currently oblivious to. You will see where you have hatreds that you are currently unaware of. You will see your fears, your constriction, and your resistance. It is disguised right now in the grand projection, the feelings you believe others cause in you. It is the terror and the sadness you feel when you look at the world. You think it is out there. You think all the death and destruction and negativities and hatefulness are outside you. You present to yourself the face of innocence because to look inside your mind is a terrifying thought for the untrained ego consciousness. Unfortunately in your society, you are relentlessly and continuously trained in fear, materialism, and attack, so the mind you think is you is a very, very small and limited version of who you actually are.

Change Your Focus to the Nonphysical

You would not believe how magnificent or loved you truly are. Most of you don't believe it. We are here to encourage you to focus on the nonphysical, and that does not mean you give up your life. It does not mean you have to live in an ashram. What it means is that when you buy your food, you think about your frequency. You think about how that food loves you, how it nurtures and nourishes you, not just how it fills you up or stuffs you or medicates you. It means when you are out walking, you do not ruminate on the material world; you look at the light. You feel your way through your environment: the wind on your face, birdsong, the trees, a babbling brook you managed to find to walk along. You are open to seeing, feeling, and communicating. It means you decide how to entertain yourself with what you think about and the frequency it holds. It means you value and love yourself each moment of each day, knowing that the things you do, think, perceive, and interact with are moment-by-moment choices. You have the choice to act from a place of expansion and love or to act from a place of contraction and fear, and each of these things is going to create that frequency in your physical structure, your body-mind complex.

If you go into the world in contraction and fear, you will contract and starve your body of the loving energy it needs to thrive. If you go into the world to love and appreciate and look for the good and the light, you will expand your energy. You will tap into levels of energy that you currently cannot tap into and see yourself as an immortal spiritual being, as consciousness existing always. It has done and always will do. In that timeless vision of yourself, you will be patient. In that timeless vision of yourself, you will be kind because you know there is no escape from your consciousness. You know everything you sow will be the harvest you reap, and you know this is the path to the kind of world and personal experience you want to have.

We encourage you to focus on the nonphysical. The material comes from these nonphysical focal points. When you focus on love and appreciation and kind thoughts and imagination and creativity, then the body, the physical world, your bank account, and the physical interactions you have with people will benefit even though you are not looking at them. Stop looking at the body and thinking it is the means to the end of what you want, and look at your heart, your inspiration, your creativity, your interest, and your passion. Know that if you focus on those nonphysical things, the physical world will take care of itself. Your earnings will come in, your body will thrive, and your relationships will be nurtured when you focus on the nonphysical because the nonphysical creates the physical. The physical world arises from the focus of your mind on the nonphysical aspects of your consciousness experience. Think about that.

Your physical body comes from what you believe and what you think about and what you say. Your physical world — your community,

142 ✳ Spirit of the Western Way

your country, and your planet — is fed by the collective, the group consciousness of all of you. If you change your mind, you will become a much more powerful creator. You will tap into realms and energies and be able to draw to you the influence of love, the most powerful force in the universe. It is the thing that holds the planets together. It is the thing that grows trees and babies. Love is consciousness gently and expansively expressing itself. It is not fear or the ego mind's tendency to destroy and attack and judge.

Know that you have everything within you in this moment to create not only the body and life you want but the world you want. Only in transforming your individual consciousness can you tap into the influence that will allow you to change the world. As long as you believe you are just a physical body with no influence (one person, one vote) and you believe in death and focus on sickness, you will get those things because you get whatever you focus on, whether you want it or not.

CHAPTER 20

The Choice Is Yours

We are Ananda, and we are your teachers. We are fellow travelers in this consciousness exploration, and we come to the end of this book with great love in our hearts and minds for this planet that you call Earth, this place you live.

Your history is very checkered, and you do not know about it. You have not been told the truth about the many civilizations and influences that have played out on your Earth plane for the many, many millennia that civilization has been growing and ebbing and flowing. You think of yourselves as the result of a few thousand years of haphazard development, but it is not that at all. Your society is the result of manipulation and control, and this is a very important principle for you to bring into your spiritual practice, into your dietary practice, and into the physical practices of your life because it is in your unconsciousness that this manipulation can continue.

It is in your unconsciousness and your willingness to be manipulated that the energetic powerhouse of your creative consciousness is harvested, but this system is coming to an end. It is coming to the end of its ability to continue because you are causing such pain and suffering through your unawareness. Many of the things you consume daily are destroying fields and valleys and families in small towns around the world because you don't know about it. You are kept in the dark by hierarchical systems that

144 ✳ Spirit of the Western Way

do not show you what they are doing. Animal life on your planet is suffering tremendously, and every time you buy a package of meat, throwing it into your shopping cart without thought, pain and suffering are perpetuated.

Understand that you are going through an energetic shift. You have decided and know instinctively that something is changing in your world and in you. This is all part and parcel of this inevitable consciousness evolution. It is not a choice anymore. If you do not join in the evolution, you will be left behind because you cannot reside in a place of high frequency when you are contaminated by low-frequency beliefs and ideas. You must cleanse yourself. You must cleanse your mind and your behaviors, but do not to be monkish. Eat healthily, choose love, and honor the planet and your brothers and sisters. You do not have to live in poverty or in a deprived way. It's quite the contrary. As you turn your televisions off, your lives will become fuller and richer and more abundant because your frequency will go up.

Because it has been programmed for so long, the mind will tell you that if you turn the television and video games off, you will suffer, but the opposite is true. It is the same story an alcoholic believes when told to stop drinking. It seems as if the world will end, but what will actually happen is the person's world will begin and flourish and open. Look at those big-screen TVs in your room, and if you want to keep them to watch movies of high frequency, then do so, but disconnect your cable, disconnect that link into the programming system that does not have your best interests at heart. If you drive a gasoline-powered vehicle, research alternatives such as hybrid vehicles. See whether you can find a used one, and see whether you can find a place that will facilitate the transition from this old and dirty system to a new one. If you are hooked into the grid and you have a few extra dollars, research grants for solar power so that you can contribute to this new world. It is in the complacency and in the unconsciousness of thinking, "This is the way it has always been, so this is the way it must be" that keeps the system going, but the system cannot continue. You are taking too much from each other, and you are having too much taken from you. There is a lack of balance and awareness, and it is not going to remain this way.

The world is changing. It is changing before your eyes, and you can see it and feel it. Plant your gardens, clean up your diet, and support clean and healthy systems, and know that when you do this, you provide for the future of your world, for the future of your grandchildren and your little nieces and nephews and your children, and you honor the loving life force that expresses on this planet.

It is always a choice, dear ones. You always have the choice between consciousness and unconsciousness. You always have the choice between love and fear, and nobody can make that choice for you. You will reap what you sow. You will feel it and live it moment by moment, but you do not need to suffer. You are the greatest creators in the world. You have the minds of gods when they are aligned with love, and that is the path to the magnificent and beautiful planet you all want to live on.

After you put this book down, look at your life. Ask, "Where can I make a little change? Where can I shift and bring more love into my life so that the frequencies of my family, my home, my body, and my world go up?" You are the creators here, dear ones; you are the minds that create this experience, so the changes must come from the mind. We have given you many prescriptions of how to shift and change your behavior, but you cannot change your behavior unless you change your mind. You cannot change your mind unless you do something to change your mind.

If you have not already, pick up *A Course in Miracles*, and begin the lessons. Begin to shift your consciousness from fear to love, from separation to communion. It is in that shift that this world will flourish into the heaven on Earth that it is capable of being. This journey is always one of separation. You will always feel that little bit of separateness from God; it is the nature of the place. But it does not have to look the way it does now. You can have community gardens, communal childcare, and egalitarian support systems, and you can work at jobs you love. These are all potentialities once you reeducate yourselves and recover from the indoctrination of the limited and limiting thought structures of your society.

We bring much joy and love to this place, but you must be receptive to feel it, and to be receptive, you must get yourselves out of fear and judgment and warring thoughts. Focus on peace, love, health, and self-realization. Be curious about your feelings, about your creativity, and about what is going on inside you. The material world does not cause your problems; your beliefs about the world cause them.

We end there, dear ones. We love you very much, and we will bring

146 ✳ Spirit of the Western Way

forth more books for you to read, more training systems for you to follow, and more light to shine in your heart and mind.

About the Author

Tina Louise Spalding was raised in a family that often visited psychics, so she is no stranger to the nonphysical world. Her channeling journey began when she settled down for a nap on the summer solstice of 2012. That afternoon, powerful energies began to surge through her body, leading to ecstasy, bliss, and an altered state of consciousness that lasted for almost a month. The feelings finally drove her to take an automatic writing workshop, where she was first made aware of Ananda. She then began to write for this group of nonphysical teachers who have come to assist us in our waking process.

Tina began channeling Jesus in the summer of 2013, when he appeared in her book *Great Minds Speak to You*. It proved to be a great challenge not only to accept the assignment he offered her — writing his autobiography — but also face many of the fears that this unusual experience brought up. Tina has been asked to channel for Jesus on an ongoing basis. Check her website, ChannelingJesus.com, for public offerings of his teachings.

Tina speaks for Ananda as a full trance channel, offering teachings and personal readings for those who seek more happiness, fulfillment, and connection with Spirit. She has dedicated her life to writing and speaking for Ananda and other nonphysical beings, sharing their wisdom and spiritual knowledge.

Light Technology PUBLISHING Presents

TO ORDER PRINT BOOKS
Visit LightTechnology.com, Call 928-526-1345 or 1-800-450-0985,
or Check Amazon.com or Your Favorite Bookstore

BY TINA LOUISE SPALDING

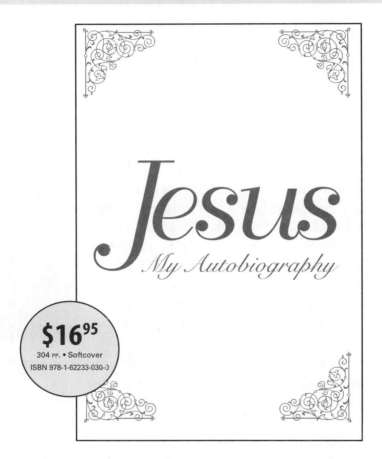

$16.95
304 pp. • Softcover
ISBN 978-1-62233-030-0

This insightful book is designed to free you from the limitations of your conditioned mind and to give you a better understanding of Jesus's life and teachings so that you can begin to transform your mind, your heart, and the world. Through Tina Louise Spalding, Jesus tells his story in his own words, clearing up misconceptions and untruths and describing his physical and nonphysical journeys that led to enlightenment.

All Our Books Are Also Available as eBooks on Amazon, Apple iTunes, Google Play, and Barnes & Noble.

Light Technology PUBLISHING Presents

TO ORDER PRINT BOOKS
Visit LightTechnology.com, Call 928-526-1345 or 1-800-450-0985,
or Check Amazon.com or Your Favorite Bookstore

by Tina Louise Spalding

Making Love to God
The Path to Divine Sex

"We have never seen more hurt and lonely people anywhere than on this planet at the moment. You are all in such a state that we have come from far and wide, from different times and places, to teach you how to relieve the deep suffering you are in. And indeed, it is in the bedroom, in your relationships to yourself, your lover, and God, that these hurts began.

"We are here to teach the way to divine bliss, and we know you are scared — scared to lie naked caressing your lover with rapt attention and honor. We know you are scared to kiss and connect, to feel such deep connection and pleasure that the ego starts to get very nervous, sensing the threat to the well-guarded and limited access to your heart that it deems to be safe.

"If we can turn the tide of thought in enough people, there will be a revolution of love on the planet, the likes of which you have never seen. Relationships will stabilize, marriages will last, and the passion and joy you so wish to experience will become manifest wherever you look."

— Ananda

$19.95   Softcover, 416 pp.
ISBN 978-1-62233-009-6

Topics Include
- How We Came to Misunderstand Sexual Energy
- Using Divine Sex Energy
- Specific Steps and Sensations
- Blocks to Transformation
- A Transformed View of Sex and Sexual Energy
- Following the Path to Transformation
- Reaping the Harvest

All Our Books Are Also Available as eBooks on Amazon, Apple iTunes, Google Play, and Barnes & Noble.

Light Technology PUBLISHING Presents

TO ORDER PRINT BOOKS
Visit LightTechnology.com, Call 928-526-1345 or 1-800-450-0985,
or Check Amazon.com or Your Favorite Bookstore

BY TINA LOUISE SPALDING

GREAT MINDS SPEAK TO YOU

With CD

"Many in spirit look on these times of difficulty, abundance, trouble, and innovation and wish to share with you their experiences and ideas. Some famous names and faces will come to mind as you read this book, and you will glean some fine information about their learning, their suffering, and indeed their experience in the life after this life, for they all wish to tell you that there is no death as you perceive it to be. They are all there in their astral forms, enjoying their continued growth, their continued expansion, and their continued joy in living.

"Read this with an open mind and heart, and hear what these beings have to say. You have revered and reviled them in life; now let them complete their stories in what you call death, for that is the complete story. Is it not?"

— Ananda

$19.95 Softcover, 192 pp.
ISBN 978-1-62233-010-2

CHAPTERS INCLUDE
- Albert Einstein
- Jerry Garcia
- Ralph Waldo Emerson
- Marilyn Monroe
- John Huston
- Amy Winehouse
- Margaret Thatcher
- Princess Diana
- Susan B. Anthony
- Sylvia Plath
- Elizabeth Taylor
- John and Robert Kennedy
- Michael Jackson
- Cecil B. DeMille
- Jonas Salk
- Queen Mother Elizabeth
- George Bernard Shaw
- Pablo Picasso
- John Lennon

All Our Books Are Also Available as eBooks on Amazon, Apple iTunes, Google Play, and Barnes & Noble.

⚛ Light Technology PUBLISHING Presents

TO ORDER PRINT BOOKS
Visit LightTechnology.com, Call 928-526-1345 or 1-800-450-0985,
or Check Amazon.com or Your Favorite Bookstore

BY TINA LOUISE SPALDING

LOVE AND A MAP TO THE UNALTERED SOUL

"True love is never-ending. It does not refuse or inflict punishment, it does not withdraw or have temper tantrums, and it does not punish. Love always is, and it always emits the same high frequency of absolute, unconditional caring and offering, of growing and creation."

— *Ananda*

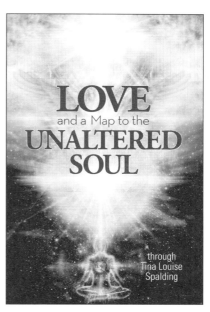

16^{95} Softcover, 192 pp.
ISBN 978-1-62233-047-8

We think we know what love is, but in *Love and a Map to the Unaltered Soul*, we are challenged to broaden our definition and free ourselves from constraints we never realized we had. In these pages, you will learn that love is a process of climbing your ladder of consciousness. Through Tina Louise Spalding, the beings Ananda, Jesus, and Mary Magdalene give practical instruction and examples on how to find and keep love at the center of your life.

CHAPTERS INCLUDE
- The Unaltered Soul Seeks Experience
- Move beyond the Physical
- You Are Part of a Greater Oneness
- You Can Raise Your Frequency
- Seek Love Within
- You Create Your Experiences
- How to Find Love
- Align with Love to Find Happiness
- Question Your Beliefs
- Implement Healthy Routines
- The Choice Is Yours
- Forgiveness Demonstrates Love

All Our Books Are Also Available as eBooks on Amazon, Apple iTunes, Google Play, and Barnes & Noble.

Light Technology PUBLISHING Presents

TO ORDER PRINT BOOKS
Visit LightTechnology.com, Call 928-526-1345 or 1-800-450-0985,
or Check Amazon.com or Your Favorite Bookstore

BY LYNN BUESS

Numerology of Astrology
Degrees of the Sun

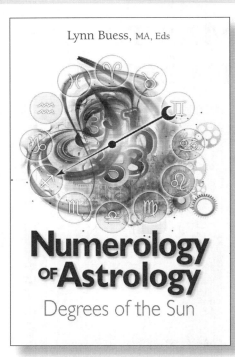

Lynn Buess, MA, Eds

$17.95 Plus Shipping
ISBN 978-1-62233-011-9
Softcover • 416 pp.

Lynn Buess has done it again! As an innovator in the consciousness and self-awareness field for over fifty years, he has now contributed a decidedly unique perspective of the time-honored system of astrology, helping humanity further understand its relationship to the universe. With this latest contribution to self-growth, Lynn offers an original perspective of numerology — this time with the combination of numerological characteristics and astrological influences. He writes not only from an intellectual viewpoint but as someone who has experienced glimpses of cosmic consciousness.

Like with most of his works, it is his hope that this volume will help seekers better connect to their cosmic memories of being both human and eternal in nature. Experience all the signs of the zodiac in minute detail:

Aries • Taurus • Gemini • Cancer • Leo
• Virgo • Libra • Scorpio • Sagittarius
Capricorn • Aquarius • Pisces

Other Books by Lynn Buess:

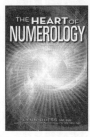
Forever Numerology
ISBN 978-1-891824-97-5
Softcover • 512 pp.
$25.30 plus shipping

Forever Numerology
ISBN 978-1-891824-65-4
Softcover • 320 pp.
$17.95 plus shipping

Numerology for the New Age
ISBN 978-0-929385-31-0
Softcover • 272 pp.
$11.00 plus shipping

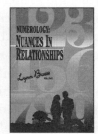
Numerology: Nuances in Relationships
ISBN 978-0-929385-23-5
Softcover • 352 pp.
$13.75 plus shipping

All Our Books Are Also Available as eBooks on Amazon, Apple iTunes, Google Play, and Barnes & Noble.

ॐ Light Technology PUBLISHING Presents

TO ORDER PRINT BOOKS
Visit LightTechnology.com, Call 928-526-1345 or 1-800-450-0985,
or Check Amazon.com or Your Favorite Bookstore

THROUGH DAVID K. MILLER

Arcturians: How to Heal, Ascend, and Help Planet Earth
Go on a mind-expanding journey to explore new spiritual tools for dealing with our planetary crisis. Included in this book are new and updated interpretations of the Kaballistic Tree of Life, which has now been expanded to embrace fifth-dimensional planetary healing methods. Learn new and expanded Arcturian spiritual technologies.
$16.95 • 352 pp. • Softcover • 978-1-62233-002-7

Kaballah and the Ascension
"Throughout Western history, channeling has come to us in various forms, including mediumship, shamanism, fortunetelling, visionaries, and oracles. There is also a long history of channeling in Kaballah, the major branch of Jewish mysticism. I am intrigued by this, especially because I believe that there is now an urgent necessity for entering higher realms with our consciousness because of the impending changes on the planet. Through these higher realms, new healing energies and insights can be brought down to assist us in these coming Earth changes." — David K. Miller
$16.95 • 176 pp. • Softcover • 978-1-891824-82-1

Biorelativity: Planetary Healing Technologies
Biorelativity describes the ability of human beings to telepathically communicate with the spirit of Earth. The goal of such communication is to influence the outcome of natural Earth events such as storms, volcanic eruptions, and earthquakes. Through the lessons contained in this book, you can implement new planetary healing techniques right now, actively participating in exciting changes as Earth and humanity come together in unity and healing.
$16.95 • 352 pp. • Softcover • 978-1-891824-98-2

A New Tree of Life for Planetary Ascension
This is the second book David Miller has written about the Kabbalah. His first book, Kaballah and the Ascension, introduced basic concepts in the Kabbalah and linked them to the ascended masters and the process of ascension. In this second book, David has teamed up with Torah scholar and Kabbalist expert Mordechai Yashin, who resides in Jerusalem, Israel. This book is based on unique lectures and classes David and Mordechai gave over an eight-month period between 2012 and 2013. These lectures on Jewish and Hebraic lessons were held in open discussion groups and offer a truly unique perspective into the Kabbalistic Tree of Life and how it has been expanded.
$16.95 • 464 pp. • Softcover • 978-1-62233-012-6

Raising the Spiritual Light Quotient
The spiritual light quotient is a measurement of a person's ability to work with and understand spirituality. This concept is compared to the intelligence quotient (IQ). However, in reality, spiritual ability is not related to intelligence, and interestingly, unlike the IQ, one's spiritual light quotient can increase with age and experience.
$16.95 • 384 pp. • Softcover • 978-1-891824-89-0

Connecting with the Arcturians
Who is really out there? Where are we going? What are our choices? What has to be done to prepare for this event? This book explains all of these questions in a way that we can easily understand. It explains what our relationships are to known extraterrestrial groups and what they are doing to help Earth and her people in this crucial galactic moment in time.
$17.00 • 256 pp. • Softcover • 978-1-891824-94-4

New Spiritual Technology for the Fifth-Dimensional Earth
Earth is moving closer to the fifth dimension. New spiritual ideas and technologies are becoming available for rebalancing our world, including native ceremonies to connect to Earth healing energies and thought projections and thought communication with Earth.
$19.95 • 240 pp. • Softcover • 978-1-891824-79-1

All Our Books Are Also Available as eBooks on Amazon, Apple iTunes, Google Play, and Barnes & Noble.

Light Technology PUBLISHING Presents

TO ORDER PRINT BOOKS
Visit LightTechnology.com, Call 928-526-1345 or 1-800-450-0985,
or Check Amazon.com or Your Favorite Bookstore

THROUGH DRUNVALO MELCHIZEDEK

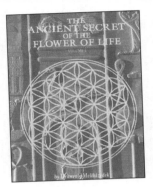

THE ANCIENT SECRET OF THE FLOWER OF LIFE
VOLUME 1

Once, all life in the universe knew the Flower of Life as the creation pattern, the geometrical design leading us into and out of physical existence. Then from a very high state of consciousness, we fell into darkness, and the secret was hidden for thousands of years, encoded in the cells of all life.

$25.00 • 240 pp. softcover • ISBN 978-1-891824-17-3

THE ANCIENT SECRET OF THE FLOWER OF LIFE
VOLUME 2

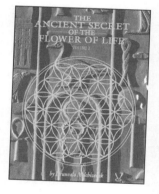

Finally, for the first time in print, Drunvalo shares the instructions for the Mer-Ka-Ba meditation, step-by-step techniques for the re-creation of the energy field of the evolved human, which is the key to ascension and the next dimensional world. If done from love, this ancient process of breathing prana opens up for us a world of tantalizing possibility in this dimension, from protective powers to the healing of oneself, others, and even the planet.

$25.00 • 272 pp. softcover • ISBN 978-1-891824-21-0

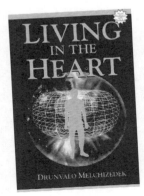

LIVING IN THE HEART

Includes Heart Meditation CD

"Long ago we humans used a form of communication and sensing that did not involve the brain in any way; rather, it came from a sacred place within our hearts. What good would it do to find this place again in a world where the greatest religion is science and the logic of the mind? Don't I know this world where emotions and feelings are second-class citizens? Yes, I do. But my teachers have asked me to remind you who you really are. You are more than a human being, much more. Within your heart is a place, a sacred place, where the world can literally be remade through conscious cocreation. If you give me permission, I will show you what has been shown to me." — Drunvalo Melchizedek

$25.00 • 144 pp. softcover • ISBN 978-1-891824-43-2

All Our Books Are Also Available as eBooks on Amazon, Apple iTunes, Google Play, and Barnes & Noble.

✦ Light Technology PUBLISHING Presents

TO ORDER PRINT BOOKS
Visit LightTechnology.com, Call 928-526-1345 or 1-800-450-0985,
or Check Amazon.com or Your Favorite Bookstore

BOOKS THROUGH ROBERT SHAPIRO

Are You a Walk-In?

From the walk-in's perspective, the benefit of this new form of birth is coming into an adult body and being able to bring one's gifts to humanity without having to take the time to go through the usual birth process. The other side of this is that the walk-in has to resolve the physical, emotional, and spiritual issues that the walk-out left behind in order to completely express its own personality.

"This book is intended to be practical advice for day-to-day living for people who know they are walk-ins, for people who believe they might be walk-ins, for the family and friends and business associates of people who are believed to be walk-ins or may believe they are walk-ins themselves. In short, this book is intended to serve the community to understand the walk-in phenomenon and for those who are experiencing it personally to be able to apply it in such a way as they are able to live easier, more comfortable, more useful, and more fulfilling lives."

— Reveals the Mysteries through Robert Shapiro

$19.95 • Softcover • 304 pp. • ISBN 978-1-891824-40-1

A New Form of Benevolent Birth Is Now Available on Earth

Zoosh, Isis, Reveals the Mysteries, and More through Robert Shapiro

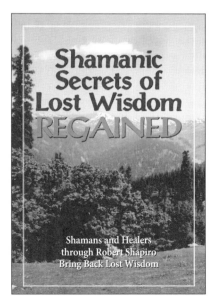

Shamans and Healers through Robert Shapiro Bring Back Lost Wisdom

Shamanic Secrets of Lost Wisdom Regained

Due to wars, natural disasters, a shaman not being able to train a successor, and many other reasons, Isis (through Robert) says that ninety-five percent of the accumulated shamanic wisdom has been lost. Now it is important to regain this wisdom as young people who are able to learn and use these processes are being born now.

Beings who lived as shamans and healers on Earth at various times now speak through Robert Shapiro and bring these lost teachings and techniques to a humanity waking up and discovering it has the talents and abilities to use this wisdom for the benefit of all.

$19.95 • Softcover • 356 pp. • ISBN 978-1-62233-049-2

All Our Books Are Also Available as eBooks on Amazon, Apple iTunes, Google Play, and Barnes & Noble.

Light Technology PUBLISHING Presents

TO ORDER PRINT BOOKS
Visit LightTechnology.com, Call 928-526-1345 or 1-800-450-0985,
or Check Amazon.com or Your Favorite Bookstore

THROUGH RAE CHANDRAN

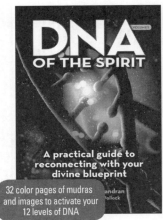

32 color pages of mudras and images to activate your 12 levels of DNA

DNA of the Spirit, Volume 1
The etheric strands of your DNA are the information library of your soul. They contain the complete history of you, lifetime after lifetime; a record of the attitudes, karma, and emotional predispositions you brought into this lifetime; and a blueprint, or lesson plan, for your self-improvement.
$19.95 • Softcover • 384 pp.
ISBN 978-1-62233-013-3

DNA of the Spirit, Volume 2
This companion book to *DNA of the Spirit, Volume 1* originated with the intention and desire to bring forth understanding to support humanity. Go through this volume while holding a sacredness inside of you, asking that the material be imprinted there so that it may become an experience that you will be able to live.
$16.95 • Softcover • 192 pp.
ISBN 978-1-62233-027-0

Dance of the Hands
Dance of the Hands is for everyone, not just people who are spiritually advanced. It is for any layperson, regardless of religion. This material is for those who have an interest in bettering themselves or improving their well-being — practitioners, teachers, masters, the spiritually advanced, neophytes, and children.
$16.95 • Softcover • 160 pp.
Wire-O bound
ISBN 978-1-62233-038-6

Partner with Angels
Angels are the Creator's workforce, and in this book, individual angels describe their responsibilities and explain how they can help you with all aspects of your life — practical and spiritual. All you need to do is ask.
$16.95 • Softcover • 208 pp.
ISBN 978-1-62233-034-8

Angels and Ascension
Angels are available with all kinds of help. This must become part of your reality. Set your antenna to the angels, and communicate with them. All of life's miracles happen with angelic presence. When you begin to do this, you will see that you have an ever-present friend at your shoulder.
$16.95 • Softcover • 128 pp.
ISBN 978-1-62233-048-5

All Our Books Are Also Available as eBooks on Amazon, Apple iTunes, Google Play, and Barnes & Noble.

Light Technology PUBLISHING Presents

TO ORDER PRINT BOOKS
Visit LightTechnology.com, Call 928-526-1345 or 1-800-450-0985,
or Check Amazon.com or Your Favorite Bookstore

BOOKS THROUGH JAAP VAN ETTEN

Birth of a New Consciousness: Dialogues with the Sidhe

This book contains the wisdom of the Sidhe, a race of human-like beings who are our direct relatives. They are invisible to our five senses and occupy one of the subtle worlds that are part of Gaia.

Embark on a journey, the journey of every soul who comes to Earth. This book stimulates you to raise your vibration and expand your view of reality by giving many suggestions on how to do so. It truly can be called the start of a new consciousness.

$16.95 • Softcover • 6 x 9 • 192 pp. • ISBN 978-1-62233-033-1

CRYSTAL SKULLS: Expand Your Consciousness

Includes 1 Meditation CD

Crystal skulls invoke a sense of mystery. What was their role in ancient times? Are they important for us now? Can they assist us on our spiritual journeys? How? Although much has been written about them, many questions linger. This book addresses these questions on practical, subtle-energy, and spiritual levels.

$25.00 • 256 pp. • Softcover • ISBN 978-1-62233-000-3

CRYSTAL SKULLS: Interacting with a Phenomenon

Discover your energetic connection with crystal skulls. Learn how to utilize these energies for your own personal growth and how these special energies affect your awareness and expand your consciousness.

$19.95 • 240 pp. • Softcover • ISBN 978-1-891824-64-7

Gifts of Mother Earth

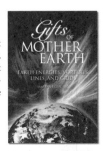

We live in a sea of energies that are part of the Earth we live on. Most people are not aware of these energies and consequently are not aware that they hold many gifts. These gifts help us to heal, balance, expand consciousness (awareness), and support spiritual evolution. Our ancestors knew the gifts of Mother Earth and used these energies to support their lives and spirituality in many ways. We, modern humans, have mostly forgotten that they exist.

$16.95 • 256 pp. • Softcover • ISBN 978-1-891824-86-9

All Our Books Are Also Available as eBooks on Amazon, Apple iTunes, Google Play, and Barnes & Noble.

SEDONA
Journal of EMERGENCE!

Find Answers to Satisfy Your Heart and Inspire Your Life in the #1 Channeled Magazine for Spiritual Guidance

YOU ARE EXPERIENCING AN UNPRECEDENTED EXPANSION into a new reality and a dimensional shift into a new state of being. There are no ancient books, rulebooks, manuals, procedures, or records of how to do this because it has never been done before.

In the *Sedona Journal of EMERGENCE!*, channeled lightbeings explain the process and offer guidance to help you feel and express love and benevolence and to encourage you to make a difference in ensuring Earth's future.

The *Sedona Journal of EMERGENCE!* is the one monthly magazine you'll want to keep on hand!
- Mine the annual PREDICTIONS issue for insights on the coming year.
- Discover channeled information and inspired guidance intended to improve your body, mind, and soul.
- Learn how to improve yourself and, by default, help the planet.

DON'T DELAY — SUBSCRIBE TODAY!
SIGN UP ONLINE AT **WWW.SEDONAJOURNAL.COM**,
CALL 1-800-450-0985 OR 1-928-526-1345,
OR EMAIL **SUBSCRIPTIONS@LIGHTTECHNOLOGY.COM**.
(ELECTRONIC SUBSCRIPTIONS AVAILABLE.)

Print Books: Visit Our Online Bookstore www.LightTechnology.com
eBooks Available on Amazon, Apple iTunes, Google Play, and Barnes & Noble

to receive SPECTACULAR SAVINGS on your *Sedona Journal* subscription!

YOU ARE EXPERIENCING AN UNPRECEDENTED EXPANSION into a new reality and a dimensional shift into a new state of being. This movement from one dimension to another while in a physical body has never been done before. It feels as if you are building the rocket you're riding while it is blasting off!

THERE ARE NO ANCIENT BOOKS, NO RULEBOOKS, no manuals or procedures, no record of how to do this thing, because it has never been done before. During previous dimensional shifts, embodied beings would die in the old reality and then be reborn in the new one in new bodies with a different vibrational frequency.

SO LIGHTBEINGS, THROUGH THEIR CHANNELS, EXPLAIN THIS PROCESS and offer guidance and spiritual techniques to help you learn to feel and express love and benevolence — and to encourage you to change your behavior to ensure that Earth remains habitable while you expand into your natural self and awaken to your natural talents and abilities. As this happens, you will allow yourself to flow with all humanity into a more benevolent version of Earth — into another dimensional focus, another of the strata of this existence.

ELECTRONIC SUBSCRIPTIONS
with Bonus Content

Get the entire journal plus additional content online by subscription — and get it 2 weeks before it hits newsstands!

❏ 2yrs........$55   ❏ 1yr..............$29

All electronic and combo subscriptions *MUST* be purchased online at www.SedonaJournal.com to obtain username and password

Get the Best of Both Worlds!
Special Combo Offers!

U.S.A.
Get BOTH Printed AND Electronic Subscriptions

1ˢᵀ Class	2ᴺᴰ Class
❏ 2yrs......$159	❏ 2yrs.........$109
❏ 1yr.........$81	❏ 1yr............$59

Canada
Get an Airmail Printed Subscription Along with an Electronic Subscription for Only

❏ 2yrs......$189   ❏ 1yr..............$99

NOTE: The U.S. Postal Service has changed postal rates, eliminating Canadian and global 2nd class surface and increasing all airmail rates.

All Countries
Get an Airmail Printed Subscription Along with an Electronic Subscription for Only

❏ 2yrs......$329   ❏ 1yr...........$170

NOTE: The U.S. Postal Service has changed postal rates, eliminating Canadian and global 2nd class surface and increasing all airmail rates.

PRINT SUBSCRIPTIONS

Mailed Subscriptions

1ˢᵀ Class	2ᴺᴰ Class
❏ 2yrs..........$129	❏ 2yrs........$79
❏ 1yr............$65	❏ 1yr..........$43

Canada

❏ 2yrs............$159   ❏ 1yr.........$83

All prices are in U.S. currency.

All Countries

❏ 2yrs............$299   ❏ 1yr.......$154

All prices are in U.S. currency.

NOTE: The U.S. Postal Service has changed postal rates, eliminating Canadian and global 2nd class surface and increasing all airmail rates.

Order online: www.SedonaJournal.com
Phone: 928-526-1345 or 1-800-450-0985

Light Technology PUBLISHING Presents
EASY ORDER 24 HOURS A DAY

Order ONLINE!
www.LightTechnology.com

Email:
customersrv@lighttechnology.net

www.LightTechnology.com
We offer the best channeled and inspired books of wisdom.
Use our secure checkout.
In-Depth Information on Books, Including Excerpts and Contents
Use the Links to Our Other Great Sites: See Below.

Order by Mail
Send To:
Light Technology Publishing
PO Box 3540
Flagstaff, AZ 86003

www.SedonaJournal.com
Read Excerpts of Monthly Channeling and Predictions in Advance.
Use Our Email Links to Contact Us or Send a Submission.
Electronic Subscriptions Available — with or without Print Copies.

Order by Phone
800-450-0985
928-526-1345

www.BenevolentMagic.com
Learn the techniques of benevolence toward self and benevolence toward others to create global peace. Download all the techniques of benevolent magic and living prayer for FREE!

Order by Fax
928-714-1132

www.ExplorerRace.com
All of humanity constitutes the Explorer Race, volunteers for a grand and glorious experiment. Discover your purpose, your history, and your future. Download the first chapter of each book for FREE!

Available from your
favorite bookstore or:

www.ShamanicSecrets.com
What we call shamanism is the natural way of life for beings on other planets. Learn to be aware of your natural self and your natural talents and abilities. Download the first chapter of each book for FREE!

Print Books: Visit Our Online Bookstore www.LightTechnology.com
eBooks Available on Amazon, Apple iTunes, Google Play, and Barnes & Noble